CLIMBING THE ROPE
TO GOD

Mystical Testimony and Teaching

The Keeneys

CONTENTS

PREFACE

After leaving our positions as university professors, we dedicated ourselves to teaching Sacred Ecstatics, our unique orientation to ecstatic spirituality. We moved to Hollywood, California, and unexpectedly began receiving visionary dreams almost every night. Each morning we wrote a report about these mystical downloads as a teaching for the students in our mentorship program. This visionary period mostly took place in Hollywood between November 2014 and April 2015, and continued afterward in other parts of the world.

The book begins with "Part One: The Formative Experiences," a glimpse of some of the key spiritual events in Brad's past, which includes meeting Hillary. That account sets the stage for "Part Two: The Hollywood Visions," a collection of written reports that offers testimony and teaching regarding the mysticism of Sacred Ecstatics. We have attempted to preserve the sequence in which the visions took place, though sometimes a report about a Hollywood vision benefits from an interspersed account of an earlier formative experience. Part Two shows the emergence of Hillary's visionary life and the way in which the mystical nature of Sacred Ecstatics became equally held in our relationship.

These "visits to the spiritual classrooms," as we call them, are ongoing and have become a primary source of our teaching and mentoring. Through these visions we and our students have been introduced to songs, symbols, and wisdom from diverse mystics, composers, poets, saints, shamans, healers, and scientists. We discuss these mystical teachings through the concepts explored at length in our foundational book, *Sacred Ecstatics: The Recipe for Setting Your Soul on Fire*.[1] Familiarity with the latter will enhance readers' understanding of this text.

The journey to the highest spiritual classroom has been called "climbing the rope to God" by the Kalahari Bushmen, one of the main lineages of Sacred Ecstatics. Holding on to this divine rope is what assures the unfolding of a sacred vision rather than a drift into psychological dream. Sacred vision is radically life-changing and inspires awe and devotion to divine mystery. All other types of dreaming involve more of the self and less of God. They should be given less attention because they empower personal inflation rather than awaken heartfelt closeness to divinity. We offer this mystical testimony and teaching as a means of pointing you toward the ultimate source and force behind creation.

Part One

The Formative Experiences

The Light in the Chapel

The following is an account of my first and most important mystical experience. It took place when I was a nineteen-year-old college student. Without question this event marked the beginning of my life as a mystic. Hillary and I both regard this as the primary reference point for our later visions, spiritual experiences, and teaching. What took place did not occur in a dream, but happened while I was fully awake.

I had previously won first place at the 1969 International Science Fair and was offered a full scholarship to the Massachusetts Institute of Technology. I delayed accepting that scholarship, however, to begin my studies at another college in Missouri. I mostly studied, played the piano, and favored listening to jazz, especially the music of Erroll Garner. I had grown up in a home with a father and grandfather who were preachers, but had no experiential familiarity with any kind of mysticism. I was simply an awkward nerd who hadn't tasted a drop of alcohol or consumed a single mind-altering pharmaceutical. I was even out of touch with the rock-and-roll times as I preferred the tunes of George Gershwin and Cole Porter played on a Steinway concert grand piano. On this January afternoon in 1971, in Columbia, Missouri, I took a walk and felt the arrival of a strange, but joyful, tingling within. I was unexplainably drawn to a small stone chapel where I entered and sat on the front pew. I suspected something big was about to happen.

A concentrated and pulsing fireball of energy gathered at the base of my spine and began to climb with a steady advance, like liquid fire flowing upward. Its ascent was accompanied by an incredible emotion that broke my heart wide open. I felt an intimacy with the divine I never knew was possible, and entered a vast ocean of love where I could not stop weeping with joy. I also noticed that my mind suddenly seemed connected to a reservoir of wisdom previously unknown to me. Above all else, however, was the burning, expanding love that kept intensifying.

My body trembled, quaked, and shook with a force that could not be called subtle, calm, or quiet. I learned firsthand that the universe has an incredible spiritual power—a sacred vibration and an electric-like current that changes your life when directly experienced. I was shocked because no one had ever told me, nor had I ever read that such a vibrant power could flow inside a human being. I was also flooded with the realization that once it is awakened it is with you forever. I knew that no matter what I would do in my life, I would be accompanied by this remarkable life force hookup.

Steadily and assuredly the inner ball of fire climbed until it reached the crown of my head and poured out as a white light. It took form in front of me and was the shape of a luminous egg that was about my height. I stared into this mysterious luminosity and, transfixed by sacred emotion, I saw a man facing me with open arms. I instantly realized that the divine son and the mystical sun of the holiest light were the same. Since then this living, mystical Jesus, whose light reformed and transformed my soul, would forever be my guide, teacher, and dwelling place.

He introduced a multisensory, multidimensional parade of innumerable saints, mystics, and spiritual teachers, one after another. Further luminous teaching was poured into me by the Virgin Mary, Our Lady of Guadalupe, the disciples, and many other major icons of religion and sacred tradition, including Black Elk, Buddha, Muhammad, Krishna . . . it seemed to never end. I literally absorbed everything I beheld. More than anything, this experience involved the intense sacred emotion of divine love. Only later was I to learn that the Kalahari Bushmen call this experience "receiving God's ostrich egg," the egg in which spiritual gifts are held and bestowed. Suffice it to say that I knew that night—and even now as I write this report over forty years later—that I was cooked by the fire and dissolved in the sea of everlasting love.

In the midst of this experience, the voice that I would forever serve, declared: "I will guide you. Follow me and the light will shine brightly . . . If you follow your reason rather than my direction, you will get lost. Fear not, for I am with you always. You shall be prepared to express these truths and share these gifts." I was warned that the journey would not be easy and that I would be no stranger to failure and suffering.

The mystical illumination continued in the chapel throughout the night and into the early morning, at least twelve hours in duration. The oval light remained visible to me for several more months, though I am not sure exactly how long because I lost track of time. What I do remember was that whenever I looked up, the light was present. During this period I often kept my head bowed for fear that if I kept staring at the mysterious light I would be swept away and never return. In truth, I never did return and nothing has ever been the same after meeting the light in the chapel.

This was the birth of my life as an ecstatic mystic. I was fully aware that I was being prepared to do something with what had been instilled inside me. I also received a foretelling that I would spend decades as a spiritual traveler, both to actual geographical places and visionary realms, in order to meet others who had been spiritually cooked in this luminous fire. All of that would come later.

In the divine light, I was initiated as an ambassador of ecstatic fire, a vibration-focused healer, a teacher of the unknowable, a numinous attendant of the luminous, and a shamanic captain who sails the musical sea. I have spent a lifetime celebrating this extraordinary mystery and experiencing its miraculous transformative power inside many places—from the Amazon to Japan, Africa, Bali, Mexico, Brazil, the Caribbean, Australia, and numerous stops in between. No matter where I went, after my first encounter with the mystery of divinity I could repeat the words of the mystic Ibn al-'Arabi and say that every word I have since uttered and written was simply "the differentiation of the universal reality comprised by that [first] look."[2]

Flying Books

Soon after that night in the chapel, while pondering whether others had similarly experienced this immersion in the spiritual fire, I went to a university bookstore. When I passed a particular aisle, a book immediately dropped off the shelf and landed on my foot. I was startled, thinking someone had pushed it toward me, but there was no one else around. It was a book written by Gopi Krishna describing his experience with what he called a "kundalini awakening."[3] This was the first time I encountered the Hindu word *kundalini*, referring to the concentrated psychospiritual energy that lies dormant within the base of the spine until awakened.

As I browsed through the book, I read that Gopi Krishna's first experience with this mysterious energy led to many painful and challenging years of symptoms before it settled. The same voice I had heard during my illumination then spoke, "You shall now be prepared to hold and articulate this gift. It is one thing to experience the holy light and another thing to host and share it in an appropriate manner. Your mind must be made ready." I closed the book and avoided following any tradition or practice, recognizing that my teacher was already giving me instruction.

That was the start of my visionary relationship with words and books. Since that time, this inner voice has faithfully guided me and served as a mystical librarian. It would often lead me to a book right at the moment that I needed to be taught something of importance. Sometimes I would dream that I was reading a passage from a book—and then accidentally come across that same book the next day and read it again while awake. These texts pointed me to many names for the luminous energy that was awakened in the chapel, including holy spirit, kundalini, *seiki*, *n/om*, universal life force, vibratory energy, and our own term, sacred vibration.

Several years later while browsing in the Arizona State University library, another book literally flew off the rack and nearly struck me on the head. I picked it up and found that it was a handmade book placed there by an anonymous donor: a translation of a treatise by a nineteenth-century eccentric scholar from Paris named Charles Henry. Initially a librarian and later a director of a laboratory at the Sorbonne in Paris, Henry proposed that what he called "vibratory energy" is the creative force behind artistic expression, and that an artist can use specific know-how about vibrations to evoke "dynamically expansive" experiences. When art is appropriately attuned to the rhythms of life, it becomes an effective medium for spreading joy. Extending this perspective to mysticism, Henry regarded the latter as the "deployment of biopsychic energy according to cosmic laws" and that mystical experience could be activated by a "therapy" capable of re-establishing "autoregulation to the biopsychic resonator."[4] He dreamed of a future form of transformative experience (articulated in his *Essai de Generalization de la Théorie de Raynonnement*) that would go past art as we know it and be a new kind of therapy or multisensory "bath," where the participant would experience a "total harmonic keyboard for the human body" based upon the principles of contrast, rhythm, and measure. This "therapy" would aim to "provoke the equivalent of an excitation of the complete nervous field, analogous to the sensation of the physiological white . . . [and] would appear to define that which literature and current language understand by the word 'love.'" He added, "the excitation of music and the appropriate locomotion, combined with that of a young perseverant, determines the nervous exaltation well known by the dervishes."[5]

Henry concluded that "there is fundamentally only one therapy"[6] and it requires a plunge into mystical light and love. Reading Henry's words deeply resonated with what I had experienced that first night in the chapel. His vision became a recurring dream for me, as I would often envision creating a special room where people could be immersed in that same luminous spiritual energy that had transformed my life. For decades I called this dreamt place "the room" and later named it the "Life Force Theatre." Hillary and I now call this mystical space "the big room" to connote a context vast enough to host the ultimate transformative experience. Sacred Ecstatics was created to foster "big room therapy" with its sacred vibration, whole body awakening, and reception of immeasurable love. Charles Henry stumbled upon important truths about the multisensory, vibrational nature of mystical experience, but fell short of realizing that exciting and uniting all the senses into the mystical light of love requires a source of inspiration beyond the human sphere. Any attempt to achieve the highest mystical experience will fail without an authentic hookup to divinity. There is simply no way to find your way to a full immersion in the mystical light without cultivating a personal, intimate relationship with the divine creator, the ultimate source of the vibration that resonates love and sets your whole life on fire.

Launched into Mystical Space

During the ten years following my illumination, I was shown how popular spirituality all over the world was largely a "carnival of the spirit," from the miraculous *siddhis* of yogis to the bizarre channeled conversations of psychics and mediums. I again and again witnessed people perform and exalt gee-whiz experiences, and saw how these primarily served the inflation of self-importance and intoxication with magical power. As my inner voice said, "How does bending a spoon, spinning a compass needle, slowing your pulse, channeling an alien, or delineating levels of consciousness ignite the soul and excite the heart with divine light and love?"

When I finally realized that it was extremely rare to find someone who had been physically and emotionally touched by the electrifying sacred vibration of divine mystery, I concluded that most of what could be found in the New Age was a spiritually impotent charade. It lacked fire, spirit, soul, and ecstasy. My inner guide stepped in and yanked me out of the carnivalesque mess, declaring that it was time for some serious academic study. In fact, I did not tell anyone about my early mystical experience for more than a decade—and I stopped playing music, assuming that it would make the mysterious light come roaring back. Instead, I immersed myself in the study of cybernetics, the science of circularly organized systems (or recursive patterns that connect and self-correct). Specializing in its application to change-oriented conversation, I became an internationally published scholar on the cybernetics of therapeutic practice.[7] After serving as research director at a renowned family therapy institute in New York City, the Ackerman Institute, I accepted a position as a tenured professor and director of a university graduate program. However, mystical experience continued to be a vital part of my life, even in academic study. I would sometimes dream a lecture before I gave it, or read an article in vision before I wrote it. Be assured that I did not disclose this to any editorial board or academic committee!

Fifteen years following my beginning illumination, I dreamed that I was ready to reactivate music for a mystical comeback. I obediently plunged into improvisational music and was not surprised to one day find myself full of the same tingling energy that had preceded my first experience. This time I was not led to a chapel, bookstore, or library, but to a public park. What differed was my impulsive invitation to a friend, a young woman and devotee of jazz and Beat poetry, to come with me. Without saying a word, we walked to a park, sat on the ground, held onto each other with a hug, and began shaking. As we shook together the fire again awakened and the divine illumination engulfed us both. Energy shot from the base of my spine and climbed to an apex, only to return and recycle as before. With each recycling, the spiritual vibration and electricity became stronger until it unexpectedly culminated in an extraordinary experience that felt like I was shot into outer space. I literally witnessed and felt myself flying through the cosmos with an ecstatic explosion of joy. It was a kind of "divine orgasm," which is how I privately coined it, that brought on a spiritual fervor and extreme heavenly delight that far exceeded carnal pleasure. I wondered whether I had discovered a secret to the universe.

I would be launched into the mystical universe like this numerous times in the years to come, never knowing when it would happen. For instance, a Guarani shaman blew into my heart when I was conducting a shamanic ceremony and I flew through the stars to land at the four original palm trees, the place of creation in the Guarani spiritual cosmos. The same happened with the Bushmen when I was launched through the galaxy to arrive at the original camel thorn tree in God's village where their original ancestors reside. Later I would discover that there are many mysteries associated with mystical ascent, whether one is shot to the stars or climbing to the heavens. The most important mystery, however, is the way every mystical journey invites even deeper surrender and brings one closer to the heart of divinity.

A Spiritual Odyssey Led by Vision

The years that followed were an ongoing exploration of how the "sacred vibration," our present name for the vibratory life force that accompanies powerful mystical experience, can be shared through interaction with others. I touched anyone who wanted to experience this vibration. I conducted improvised shamanic ceremonies, spiritual services, healing rituals, experimental theatre events, and all kinds of encounters, doing so as an open-minded exploration of how this vibration and electricity could be transferred and shared.

Visions poured through me often and I would receive a phone number or map that led me to many spiritual elders around the world, from the Lakota, Ojibwa, Cree, Diné, and Micmac Indians, to Japan, Bali, Africa, the Amazon, and other places. I was invited to be a deacon in a sanctified African American church where I worshipped on Wednesday nights and Sundays, while secretly conducting spirit-calling meetings for numerous medicine men and women who requested a healing from me. I seemed to have a direct phone line to mystery and received my marching orders, travel itineraries, and professional contacts in dream.

As I was admitted to the healing rites of diverse indigenous traditions of North America, their elders, especially those associated with the American Indian Movement, recommended that I keep my involvement a secret for a long while because others would never be able to understand or accept that the Creator doesn't care about skin color. These elders weren't concerned about sharing spiritual "secrets" with me because, like

Frank Fools Crow, they believed that "[t]he ones who complain and talk the most about giving away Medicine Secrets, are always those who know the least."[8] However, there is also wisdom in not disclosing all the details about certain mystical matters because they simply cannot be understood by those without a strong divine hookup, and therefore might cause a distraction or short-circuit in someone's spiritual development.

I was aware of many so-called "plastic white shamans" as well as "plastic natives" who made up their reports of spiritual experience, had no strong working relationship with spirit, and couldn't distinguish actual mystical experience from wishful thinking. There is equal capacity for inauthenticity, confusion, and ignorance among people of all skin colors and cultural backgrounds, and this applies to both spiritual practitioners and their critics. I have witnessed indigenous people carelessly incorporate ideas from the New Age, psychotherapy, and psychology into traditional ways, not realizing how this unnecessarily pollutes and often altogether negates old wisdom. I have also observed bestselling authors of all colors and stripes make irresponsible claims that amount to nothing but selling snake oil. I have met several spiritual pop stars and was shocked that the public could fall for their trite messages and blatantly obvious con jobs. While most people acknowledge that there will always be charlatans, they still remain gullible when a sales pitch promises quick and easy access to their personal fantasy of whatever spiritual tradition strikes their fancy.

I was — and still am — clearly aware of the hustlers who litter the New Age marketplace with outright lies, and how these frauds make it easy for a critic to overgeneralize that every contemporary shaman and teacher is a fake. However, this criticism adds nothing new to what is already obvious, and irresponsibly throws out any innocent baby with the dirty bath water. What we desperately need are anointed wisdom teachers *and* anointed wisdom critics, both working together to help build sacred ground for everyone. We also need to be careful about making spirituality a condition of cultural identity. The real problems of historical oppression and racism are too easily eclipsed by a hyperfocus on the more-than-obvious idiocy and ineptitude of a nonindigenous outsider offering a half-baked commercialized imitation of indigenous spirituality. It deeply troubled many of the indigenous wisdom keepers I knew that activists too often overlooked what would have been a better battle: fighting for the equal rights of all medicine people to receive the same benefits and participation in the health care system as allopathic physicians. Fighting over who gets to wear feathers and beads pales in comparison to the more important social and economic struggle for the equal acceptance and support of all traditional medicine.

Someone spiritually cooked and anointed is better qualified to make a sound spiritual judgment concerning who is a spiritual imposter and who is not; this requires spiritual rather than political discernment. We unfortunately live in a time when questions of spiritual and cultural appropriation are easily confounded and inappropriately handled through the limited precepts of political ideology rather than the vaster wisdom of holy people whose primary allegiance is to the highest realm. We must guard against how both spiritual charlatanism and a political activist critique of the latter may distance people from the Creator, leading to impoverished disputes within and across cultural groups.

I have felt equally alienated from the spokespeople of neo-shamanism — the neon sign shamans — as well as the antagonistic culturists who believe that their cultural heritage, rather than spirit, grants them entitlement to do holy work and act as its gatekeepers. There is no entitlement to spiritual work — it's neither self-appointed, culturally inherited, socially granted, nor purchased. It comes from the Creator. It also matters not whether the healer or teacher is gifted with paper money, groceries, a car, or a couple of horses or mules (as the payment sometimes was in the past). Everything about spiritual work, including the nature of gifts and exchange, should reside under the roof of the Big Holy,[a] which usually means that the specific details will be different for each person.

Elders of diverse cultural groups personally encouraged me to continue on, and warned that it would be hard because I would have to endure both the jealousy of plastic shamans and the disdain of those who could not accept that a white person can have any real and respectful relationship to indigenous religions. Again, authentic medicine people value spiritual anointment and follow divine direction, even if it means welcoming an outsider into their sacred space. Their trust lies in the higher discernment handed down by the Creator, not in the limited understanding of human beings. In the infinite realm of divine mystery, one finds that music, dance, and prayers are not restricted by manmade boundaries. They are under the rein of the Creator, freely distributable through the divine rope that is guided and regulated by a higher will.

One night I awakened to find a circle of old Lakota medicine men in my room. They looked like ghosts as they sang and handed me a pipe and drum. At another time, I was taken inside the shaking tent and given its rattle and pipe. On another night I was conversing with Persian mystics or sharing bread with a former Christian mystic. These visions shook the core of my being. They left me trembling with an extra boost of spiritual

---

[a] This term comes from Luther Standing Bear in his book, *Land of the Spotted Eagle* (Lincoln: University of Nebraska Press, 1933). Standing Bear writes: "The Indian loved to worship. From birth to death he revered his surroundings. He considered himself born in the luxurious lap of Mother Earth and no place was to him humble. There was nothing between him and the Big Holy. The contact was immediate and personal, and the blessings of Wakan Tanka flowed over the Indian like rain showered from the sky" (256).

energy and refilled my heart with ecstatic joy because they brought me closer to God.

I was a professor teaching innovative psychotherapy at the university by day and a mystic by night. In my academic work I was bringing mystical knowledge to therapeutic practice without saying I was doing so. I confess that I was disappointed, confused, and heartbroken to find that thunderous applause for a clinical session conducted at a professional conference could also inspire banishment due to professional jealousy. For instance, at an international conference on psychotherapy in Sao Paulo, Brazil, where many renowned therapists were presenting, I saw a family with a teenage boy whose sporadic convulsions neither medical science nor psychotherapy could cure or understand. In a session lasting less than forty minutes, the family was transformed, resulting in the audience of hundreds standing on their feet cheering and weeping. Several of the famous therapists in attendance immediately asked for private sessions and afterward expressed personal gratitude for a change in their own condition.

Later that week all the invited presenters sat behind tables, available to sign their books. I was the youngest presenter, but the emotion stirred by my clinical session had resulted in a very long line formed by people wanting to meet me. Practically no one was in line to meet the other presenters. I looked at my older colleagues and wondered whether my career would be over. I heard later that week from the conference co-organizers that some of the leaders of psychotherapy had privately demanded that I never be invited back to such a conference.

This kind of alienation took place over and over again as my work was denigrated for going beyond the boundaries of therapy. At this point, I had told no one of my spiritual life. Still, those who called my work creative and masterful did so not as a compliment but as a disqualification, saying that it was beyond the reach of students and too difficult to teach or replicate. I once heard a director of a psychotherapy institute in Buenos Aires tell an audience that my clinical work was not legitimate therapy because I was clearly a shaman. That's when I decided I might as well go public and announce that I actually was a shaman.

Within months after my coming out of the shaman's closet, I dreamed I was to attend a private gathering in upstate New York. After the dream I received an invitation to co-conduct a ceremony there with a young elder of the Kogi Indians who had just arrived from the Sierra Nevada de Santa Marta Mountains of northern Colombia. We exchanged the eagle and condor feathers while sitting in a circle of spiritual members from many faiths. I recall blowing a puff of air that lifted both feathers off the floor as we watched them dance in midair. I felt like Forrest Gump of the spirit world; I seemed to randomly show up at places and conduct ceremonies that often crossed the boundaries of diverse spiritual traditions.

I once experienced a waking vision in the middle of the night in which I was told to go out outside, only to find Mt. Fuji in my backyard. I climbed it and met one of my Japanese teachers who gave me *seiki*, an old Japanese name for the nonsubtle life force. I wondered whether that vision explained why Ikuko Osumi Sensei[b] had years before given me a painting of that mountain, only saying, "Someday you will climb it."

In another visionary experience I met a star in the sky that transformed into a nun whose name was Sister Elize. To my surprise, a week later I actually found her painted image on the living room wall of one of the great Zulu healers of our time, Mama Mona Ndzekeli. When I told her this, Mama Mona said, "That is my main spirit guide. Now go outside and walk around

---

[b] The late Ikuko Osumi, Sensei was one of the strongest healers of 20th Century Japan. She practiced *seiki jutsu,* the art of the vital life force. I lived with Osumi Sensei for several years and she passed on her lineage to me in 1996. For more information, see our book, *Seiki Jutsu: The Practice of Non-Subtle Energy Medicine* (Rochester, VT: Healing Arts Press, 2014).

my house. Say a prayer and then come back." I followed her instruction, and as I was walking I noticed three small stones on the ground. I picked them up, and after seeing that each had an image drawn on them, I placed them in my pocket. When I came back to Mama Mona's chapel, she asked what happened. I showed her the three stones and she screamed, "My God, those are the healing stones! Many years ago during my initiation ceremony, I was mysteriously led to them after I walked through a swamp filled with crocodiles. The elders in my village said, 'Ancestral spirits choose who will receive the stones. When it is time for you to leave this life, the stones will be given to someone else.'" Months before the stones had disappeared from Mama Mona, and now I was holding them. In a ceremony, she and her husband transferred "all the spirits and guides of Africa into my body," which is how they described it. I felt overwhelmed and dizzy from experiencing what seemed like a fast-motion movie of birds, animals, creatures, spirits, and forces.

This kind of thing happened over and over again. I would be led to healers, mystics, shamans, and teachers who claimed to download their spiritual power, knowledge, and guides into me. It was like the sky was raining cats and dogs as well as South Dakota eagles and African crocodiles. After being gifted with the remaining hair of a Tibetan rainmaker, allegedly left behind when he went rainbow body, an old medicine man gave me an explanation of what was taking place, doing so with a grin. He said, "The reception of these blessings is akin to the art of making it rain. It's about having a knack for showing up at the right time."

During this time I was introduced to a professional head-hunter who had been the former director of the Educational Testing Service at Princeton. He was looking for someone who a wealthy client might want to sponsor. Weeks later I was flown to Philadelphia and asked to propose any kind of project for them to consider funding. This meeting launched my decade-long career traveling the world visiting healers, shamans, and spiritual teachers to collect first-person accounts of their lives and traditions. I privately said that I was a "secretary to the elders," helping endangered cultures conserve whatever wisdom they wished to protect. This resulted in the encyclopedic Profiles of Healing series.[9]

I could go on and on about how I went from one village and continent to another, living full-time as an ecstatic mystic guided by vision. What is more important is the fruit of that labor, which contributed to the conservation of ancient healing wisdom in print as well as audio and video recording. A decade later, I had a vision of being in a canoe on a sea of glass, accompanied by many of the elders with whom I had lived. When the boat came to shore, I got out and turned around to see an audience waiting for me to teach. I knew that my odyssey around the world had come to an end. It was time for me to share what the mystical egg had first delivered and what years of polishing a cybernetic mind and journeying to meet others who work the spirit had taught me. Not long after that vision I met Hillary; we soon married and dedicated ourselves to Sacred Ecstatics. Before telling that story, though, there are a few more formative experiences that are important to share.

Further Experimentation

For over ten years, with foundation support, I was able to be largely removed from modern culture and live in remote places where ecstatic spirituality was a long-established way. When I made an occasional appearance in the world of psychotherapy or at New Age venues, I was disappointed and sad to be reminded of the paucity of knowledge concerning ecstatic experience and how to host the sacred vibration should it awaken. For a while I reluctantly allowed people to have their way with the spiritual current that came through me. I felt like a spiritual prostitute. I trusted that this approach was a way of teaching me more about the world's relationship to mystery, but I pleaded with God to release me from this duty. I would sometimes go all day and all night as a line of over 500 people would wait, wanting to get zapped by a hit of spiritual energy.

I wasn't like the teachers or healers who only briefly touch, allowing people's imagination to trigger a placebo response. Instead, I shook with the sacred vibration and sweated profusely, chanted loudly, and danced wildly as I hooked people up to nonsubtle life force and spiritual electricity. I was a spiritual gas station: "Fill 'er up!" Strange things happened in this work. Light bulbs exploded, microphones sometimes caught fire, lightning struck buildings, fires spontaneously started, and the like. I recall that after one handheld microphone blew up, the sound engineer put a lapel microphone on me and it, too, started to smoke. Once at the crescendo of a healing session, the fire alarm went off in the conference center for no explainable reason.

In the early days of this experimentation, my science-trained mind was sometimes curious to tinker with this mysterious power in all kinds of less-than-holy ways. I once energetically focused on a large sum of money and it came the next week. Believing it might be a coincidence, I tried it again, this time making it a larger amount, and it also appeared. My inner voice advised me to stop because I had learned enough. Later, I tried imagining meeting a couple at a certain spot at noon in the middle of the street in front of a particular building in New York City. I had only seen this couple once and didn't even know their names. Sure enough, I went to that spot and they showed up right on time.

Once again, I knew this experimental tinkering had to stop, along with the other explorations that only fed my curiosity. In the surprises and mishaps of these experiments I learned firsthand how the offerings from illumination could bring *siddhis*, at the price of perpetuating the trickster teachings of New Age and New Thought gurus who claim that spirituality is about magically manifesting your personal will and desires. While the latter popular teaching is totally exaggerated and oversimplified to sell books and workshops to the masses, in the hands of someone spiritually cooked, such magic is sometimes possible, but the cost may be the loss of the very power that brought it about. The spiritual concern is that the pursuit of personal power and magic takes your eyes off of God, causing you to drift farther and farther away from higher mystery.

I also discovered how people could project their fantasies onto me and bring forth both actual physical outcomes as well as illusory hallucinations, derived from the way their wishes and desires mixed with a lust for spiritual power. If you make yourself a well-prepared empty vessel or hollow tube, authentic spiritual experience can take place in the midst of a heightened spiritual energy field. I worked with Tibetan monks who experienced the mystical white light and Christian preachers who felt God touch them or arrive that night in a dream. On the other hand, a group of psychoanalysts who believe that everyone is organized by repressed libidinal energy might spontaneously have an orgasm, which happened with a group of therapists I taught in Belo Horizonte, Brazil. The outcomes were even crazier following New Age presentations, when people sometimes claimed that afterward I appeared as a luminous form in their houses or that I had done unusual magical things to them. Bizarre reports like this were not uncommon.

At one conference, the audience became so delirious with ecstatic energy that one person shouted out, "He has ripped apart the ectoplasmic shield!" Half the audience fled while the other half charged the stage. It seemed the entire auditorium had turned into a spaceship and gone into orbit. This also took place in classrooms at universities where students reported they had had been transported through a portal into another reality. Several students once claimed I had reached my hand through the blackboard and opened the wall for them to be sucked into another dimension. This confused and sometimes disturbed me as I witnessed how people's trickster mind filtered and interacted with the mystical light to produce a refracted ray that was bent away from the highest illumination. To put it differently: I found that a person's most primary desires and beliefs could be made experientially real inside a situation that radiated highly amplified spiritual energy, similar to the effect of taking a hallucinogen. The software of a person's mind seemed to program the experienced reality that emerged whenever energetic excitation took place.

I sought deeper refuge in cultures that had more expertise and wisdom in hosting divinely inspired ecstatic expression. I was reassured when Osumi Sensei watched me give the amplified life force, called *seiki*, to over one hundred people, including her daughter. I also felt the natural normality and goodness of this work when I transmitted *n/om* to many Bushman *n/om-kxaosi*[c] in Botswana and Namibia. As I felt more and more at home in these places, I felt less and less at home in my culture of origin. I longed for a community that could hold up sacred ground and foster climbing the rope to God.

This was about the time when the divine illumination, the mystical egg, began schooling me in the secrets of the dark, as I found that the darkest evil shows up wherever the brightest light shines. I went through years of having death threats put on my life and other attacks that arose from the Christian religious right-wing element, a coven of witches, power-hungry shamans,

---

[c] The healers or doctors among the Bushman (San) people of the Kalahari region of southern Africa are called *n/om-kxaosi*, which literally translates from the Ju/'hoan language as "owner" or "possessor" of *n/om*. The term *n/om* refers to the spiritual power or life force that fills the body of a doctor during a healing dance and is transmitted to others for the purposes of healing and spiritual awakening. Transmission is typically described as receiving a thorn, arrow, or nail of *n/om*. See our book, *Way of the Bushman: Spiritual Teachings and Practices of the Kalahri Ju/'hoansi* (Rochester, VT: Bear & Company, 2015).

scorned New Age seekers whose humanness had been exposed, Navajo skin walkers, scary beings, and other forces of evil from both the natural and the so-called supernatural world. I have previously written about my all-night scare with the god of the *balians* (shamans) in Bali and of facing creatures that came to suck the life and materiality out of me.[10] I have said less about casting out demons, exorcising towns, and nearly losing my life while engaged one way or the other in dealing with dark forces, spirits, and entities. Finally, after these impossible-to-comprehend things settled down, I was taught how they work, and how to recognize and deal with them. Ultimately this comes down to not paying any attention to them, by remaining in the strongest core of the light. Hence, I will say nothing more about it. Let us simply celebrate and proclaim that the divine is the holy light of the world, and though you may sometimes walk through the valley of the shadow of death, you will fear no evil when the light is by your side.

I eventually made my way to the Caribbean island of St. Vincent. There I was spiritually washed clean and reborn in their mourning ceremony. In mystical vision and in their spiritual community, I became re-anointed with the specific appointment to heal, work the spirit, teach, and minister. On that island I fully appreciated and accepted that there is only one main teaching: you must become a sunbeam for God and point others to the holiest source of illumination. My years of learning how easy it is for others to be distracted and lost by the promises of power and magic gave me more compassion and renewed zeal to invite everyone to hold onto the main rope to God. Don't waste your life dabbling with lower spiritual desires and pursuits, and don't merely window shop and avoid going through the door. Grab hold of the divine rope and allow the highest power to reel you in, work on you, and make you ready for whatever mission you are meant to fulfill.

Looking back at this odyssey — it was over 46 years ago when

I saw the light in the chapel—I marvel at how thick-headed and armored I must have been to have taken so long to graduate from mystery school. At the same time, I continue to visit the visionary classrooms and never know when the next lesson will come. After dreaming the visionary canoe, however, I knew it would soon be time to teach the all-but-lost ways of ecstatic spirituality. I was also aware that almost every spiritual teacher I had ever met had passed on. I was simply getting older and time was running out.

With the wise counsel of an Ojibwa holder of medicine, I had long ago decided to require at least three visions to help filter the more important and seasoned visions from the fledgling ones. If I didn't vision something three times, I was more reluctant to immediately take action, unless of course there was an exceptional intensity to the vision. It was now becoming exceedingly clear that it was time for this ecstatic work to be placed in the world.

Though my grandfather had always wanted me to be a minister, I was cautious about such a role for the church had, in my father's words, "killed my grandfather." The bickering that took place among church deacons and parishioners, especially with regard to interpreting "the word" of the Bible, got to him and after one heated deacon's meeting he had a cerebral stroke. My father subsequently became angry at both the church and God, and was soon on his way to becoming an alcoholic. Let's say that I was not in any hurry to accept any kind of ministerial role. Furthermore, I had already repeatedly found out how easy it was for people to become angry and viciously aggressive whenever their cherished beliefs were stretched or changed in any way. As Hillary and I sometimes both joke and lament to each other, it doesn't take much to piss off a Christian if you mention New Age metaphors, and it is just as easy to enrage a New Ager with any kind of religious talk, especially if it is associated with Christianity. The open, changing, and expanding experiential realm of a mystic assuredly gets you ex-communicated by everyone. To be a minister of a syncretic, constantly transforming, mystical, ecstatic, First Creation religion is not something anyone would want to rush into!

Having personally witnessed the irrational meanness that people can enact in either the name of religion or anti-religion, I was hesitant to hang up any sign or set up a tent anywhere. I had to get so spiritually cooked that my heart could rise above any surrounding pettiness and not be tempted by either despair or anger. During the many private gatherings, workshops, and events I used to conduct, I'd close my eyes and imagine standing on the Kalahari sand or on another spiritual campground. I was learning to stand in the big sacred room—no matter where I was physically located.

Tequila Prophet

After working for several years with traditional healers and *curanderos* around the city of Oaxaca in Mexico, they took me to one of their most respected spiritual elders, a farmer who lived in the countryside. After he did his prayers and tests, he said to my hosts, "You must take him to the head priest." He was insistent and meant that I should be taken to a high-ranking priest in Oaxaca, a man I assumed was like some kind of bishop or official in the church. We immediately drove to the city and the next day went to a senior priest of the Catholic Church for that area. Accompanied by his colleagues, he interrogated me for the entire morning and afternoon. "What was your first vision? What do you believe?" and then more "what about this?" and "what about that?" I wondered whether they thought I was evil and needed to have demons cast out of me. I prayed and sang quietly to myself the first song my grandparents and parents had taught me: "Jesus loves me, this I know, for the Bible tells me so; Little ones to him belong; They are weak, but he is strong. Yes, Jesus loves me!"

At the end of the questioning, the inquisitors left the sanctuary and went to their office. I sat in the chapel remembering how I had sung this same children's song during a peyote meeting held on the Navajo Reservation. A gathering of medicine people who preside over this rite invited me to a special meeting where, unbeknownst to me, I would be tested. Prior to that, in vision I had been given sacred songs of their elders and shown things outsiders were never allowed to see. I had also received the blessing to be a conduit for their holy ways, something unimaginable for a foreigner to be granted. At first this resulted in spiritual attacks on me that included a strange beast knocking on the window of my house in the middle of the night. You can imagine my fright when I looked out the window and saw an orange and green creature staring at me. Within minutes I received a phone call from a Diné medicine woman who lived over 500 miles away, asking, "Did you see it too?"

Soon a group of Diné elders wanted to put me on another testing ground. One of them was a surviving Navajo code breaker who had met the president of the United States after a movie, "Windtalkers," was made about the contribution he and his colleagues made in World War II.[11] Let us say these elders were not warm and kind at first; they showed up ready to eradicate anyone not belonging in their community. Had I known that, I likely would not have gone. I only went because my inner voice and guide instructed me to attend. I also had never taken a mind-altering plant substance, so this test was out of my comfort zone. I sat inside the tipi and internally sang the same song, "Jesus Loves Me," as the peyote was administered. I was supposed to feel something or at least get sick, but I felt nothing. They upped the dosage; we ate buttons, powder, and liquid forms. The medicine woman presiding over the ritual finally leaned over and whispered to me, "You need to have a vision." She then gave me what I later found out was jimson weed to smoke, which has a substance that is supposed to quickly induce hallucination. I still felt nothing.

More plant medicine was administered, and the medicine woman said more loudly into my ear, "You need to have a vision because everyone here is getting sick." Sure enough, all the participants, each of them a Peyote Roadman, had become very ill. I kept on privately singing to myself and asked God to give me a vision so this situation could be resolved. Within seconds, I experienced myself jump into the fire and become a lion. I roared at everyone, communicating something in a language I didn't understand, and then sang an unfamiliar song. That's when the others started weeping and asking for forgiveness. They apologized and said they had not entered into this ceremony with a clean heart. They offered their brotherhood and sisterhood, mentioning that after seeing the startling transformation, the song that followed touched their hearts.

As I sat in the chapel in Oaxaca, it felt similar to being in that peyote ceremony where I was x-rayed by scrutinizing eyes. When the head priest returned, he announced, "After praying about these things I am certain that I know what you are. You are a prophet like the prophets of the Old Testament. We give you our blessing and pray that you continue following God's calling for your life. May this be a blessing to others as it has been to us today." After that evaluation by a respected Catholic priest, the local healers wanted me to live in Mexico. Several weeks later, a carload of them drove across the desert and as they were driving, they saw a bright light along the side of the road. They pulled over and walked toward it. All of them swore that they saw an illumined Jesus, standing in a bright light. They could only see his feet in sandals as the rest of him was simply an orb of light. He then walked away and vanished into thin air. Afterward, the healers drove straight to where I was staying and asked that I make this my home because something very important was spiritually unfolding in Mexico. "God made you a prophet to help us," one of the men suggested.

I only told a few people about what took place in Mexico. I would often conclude my story by teasing, "That's how I became the tequila prophet!" It was too much to take too seriously, and a bit of absurdity helped my humanity reckon with something much bigger than my capacity to understand. If pressed to say what I thought had taken place in all these situations, I would say that others could simply discern that I was not alone. The luminous egg was around me, beside me, and inside my heart. This was my biggest truth and only a few could see it. Even fewer knew how tired and weary I was trying to live and work amidst the chaos of trickster-bound spiritual seekers and the impoverished helping professions. I wished I could find a peaceful homecoming.

Let Us Pray Inside the Lord

In spite of my caution about the church and other institutions — knowing what the church had done to my father and grandfather — I continued to receive the call to minister. Years after what had happened in Mexico, I went to a strong spiritual classroom where I was inside a sanctified church. I was preaching and a prayer spontaneously came out of my mouth. "Let us pray inside the Lord . . ." I was so struck by the prayer that I woke up trembling. I actually jumped out of bed and entered the rest of the prayer and sermon into a Google search. A PBS website popped up with a story and video clip about a "circuit rider,"[12] an old-fashioned itinerant preacher who travels from one small town to another, handling several churches each Sunday. This practice started in nineteenth-century America, when they rode on horseback rather than traveled by automobile. My grandfather did this when he was a young preacher, first traveling by horseback and later by car as an evangelist. The circuit rider is a vanishing breed, and no one knows how many are still around.

The circuit rider in the website story was Pastor Brown. He

drove an old Chevy and pastored seven churches in Louisiana and Mississippi. He preached with the words I had delivered in my visionary church: "I been sometimes up, sometimes down, sometimes right, sometimes wrong, but I go to somebody. He takes me in his arms. He rocks me when I'm weary. He tells me that I'm his own. Oh, he's all right. He's all right."[13]

I continued to read the article. Pastor Brown barely made enough money to pay his bills, but he kept preaching. "I come to tell you that the world's greatest need is God. Not gold but God. Not silver but salvation. Not lumber but love. Not gas but grace."[14] I was trembling and shaking as I read his words. I had heard them that night in the classroom and felt them come out of my mouth. I was then jolted with surprise as I read the last paragraph and discovered that Pastor Brown lived near me. He was actually a neighbor living several blocks away in Monroe, Louisiana. Before long I was driving Pastor Brown to some of his churches along the Mississippi Delta. He told me his story and encouraged me to step even further inside God's calling. Within a year after our meeting, Pastor Brown passed away and I was left longing for a driving companion and spiritual associate.

The Missing Link: Hillary

The many different pieces of the giant spiritual puzzle I had gathered for over forty years could not have been put together without Hillary. She had also grown up as a kind of intellectual nerd who early on read philosophy, wrote poetry, and studied dance. She had the advantage of extraordinary teachers at Cranbrook, a renowned private school she attended near Detroit, Michigan. Hillary accepted a full scholarship to Vassar College, but before she began a tragic automobile accident killed her father, brother, and grandmother, and she was left with only her mother. This shock to a close-knit family left her suspended over the existential abyss. Her promising academic career was interrupted as she went into a tailspin.

Most surprising to Hillary was that in the moment the news of the accident was delivered, she experienced what can only be described as the veil of her known reality lift, delivering a felt sense of vastness, completeness, and total absence of fear. She was surprised, and a bit confused, that in the midst of this heartbreak she was also filled with a pervading feeling of freedom and peace. Hillary shared this with no one, though this feeling stayed with her for many months following the accident, despite the simultaneous confusion and challenge of starting adulthood amidst such turmoil. Immediately thereafter, at the age of eighteen, Hillary randomly picked up a book on Buddhism from her friend's bookshelf, and its message that suffering and spiritual awakening go hand in hand resonated with her deeply. This teaching gave context and a kind of spiritual legitimacy to her experience.

Hillary made her way back to the university and studied dance at the University of Michigan and the University of Colorado. During college she became more interested in academic topics that were concerned with social justice and transformation, which is what led her to major in women's studies. As a high school student Hillary had studied philosophy and literature for the delight of intellectual curiosity. Immediately after the accident, however, the same philosophical books now smelled stale; she could discern that although the authors conveyed complex ideas, they were not in relationship to the vastness that had become her undeniable compass. With her heart now opened, Hillary's life became more concerned with the spiritual pursuit of relating to suffering and the bare truth of existence, and for this reason she found a home inside Zen Buddhism. It took years of wondering and wandering to make her way to the Zen Center of Los Angeles, where she lived during the day — often dancing in the salsa and tango clubs at night. Later when Hillary encountered cybernetics and my book, *Aesthetics of Change*,[15] it was her grasp of Zen that gave her the bridge to its circular ideas and paradoxes. Our meeting reignited her passion for scholarship.

We were assigned to co-teach a course at the California Institute of Integral Studies, based in San Francisco, and the week that the course began the students hosted an evening ecstatic event where I could introduce shaking medicine. Without my knowing it, Hillary entered the dark room and sat down. With closed eyes, I spontaneously walked to her and placed my hand on her head. I felt immediately transported to the Kalahari and recognized the vibration that came when I touched their strongest *n/om-kxaosi*. We held on to one another in the middle of that gathering for hours. When someone turned the light on and I saw it was Hillary, I knew she and I would never separate and forever be partners in this teaching mission.

Later when I took Hillary to meet the Bushman elders, they also felt what I had experienced with her. She carried the sacred vibration, spiritual softness, and illumined heart recognized by spiritually cooked ecstatics. Over the subsequent years, I witnessed Hillary absorb the teachings it had taken me decades to gather. It was like watching a fast-speed film of a journey into the heart of the divine, absent of distraction and unnecessary noise. The first Buddhist name she had received was "Empty Temple," and I feel that name is apt.[d] She was already prepared to receive transmission of the ecstatic lineages. For five years, she was immersed in ecstatic experience and teaching. After she was sent to various spiritual classrooms, she was able to host the sacred vibration, amplify it, and give it to others. She first transmitted *seiki* to a Brazilian engineer who walked away so spiritually intoxicated that he passed out and slept for nearly twelve hours. Her spiritual discernment had already been present before we met, but it was now super-charged with

---

[d] This name was given to Hillary from Haju Sunim at a Korean Buddhist center in Ann Arbor, Michigan.

ecstatic energy. She undisputedly became the holder of the diverse lineages associated with our way of helping others get spiritually cooked. We were brought together to teach through relationship and the complementary dance of our mutually entwined ropes to God.

The Mojo Doctors

Just as Hillary and I began our life together in Louisiana, I published a book titled *The Flying Drum: The Mojo Doctor's Guide to Creating Magic in Your Life.*[16] It includes stories of sessions I conducted in which spiritual mystery and objects helped touch and transform people's lives. With Hillary's encouragement, I chose the title metaphor "mojo doctor" because it reflected my desire to leave behind any association with psychotherapy and instead contextualize our work in the more creative and spiritually rich helping traditions of the Deep South, where we lived.

Hillary and I got engaged in Rio de Janeiro, where we were teaching. That same week we received an email from someone offering to help support our work. He had previously financially supported the introduction of meditation to the West through his large contributions to the Transcendental Meditation (TM) movement. After feeling frustrated by the greed associated with its leader, he became discouraged for many years. He had made a prayer asking that if there was any person he should help, then he needed to receive a spiritual sign the next day. He proceeded that morning to go to a bookstore in Boulder, Colorado. There he found my book sticking out of a shelf in the wrong place, in a section that had nothing to do with spirituality. He immediately purchased the book and after reading it that night, he woke up with his heart feeling like it was on fire. That's when he contacted us to help with our teaching.

He met us in Phoenix, Arizona the following week and asked how he could support us. We suggested that we simply wanted to share our teaching with others, but we wanted to avoid the clichéd New Age centers such as Santa Fe, Sedona, and other high mountain places, and instead head to the muddy water and swamps near the Mississippi River. We suggested several places, including New Orleans. We thought that soulfulness thrived there, as well as the wisdom of holy absurdity and the rhythms of vibrant life. With his help, we set ourselves up to be "the mojo doctors" in a shop on Chartres Street in the French Quarter. We designed it to look like a shamanic cabaret, outfitted with a Steinway concert grand piano, vibrant mystical and theatrical paintings on the walls, Persian carpets on the floor, and an altar of sacred objects that were close to our hearts. We were ready to teach the world in this spiritual harbor of the Crescent City.

We spent several months practicing as local mojo doctors in New Orleans and had fascinating sessions with those who dropped by our intriguing place. The week before our first teaching event, I woke up in the middle of the night thinking that perhaps this setting was not the best way to introduce our work. I wondered whether we should instead be more like old-school healers and teachers who welcomed clients and students to their homes. I remembered all the spiritual elders around the world I had been with, and how people went to their homes to receive healing and teaching. I had no idea what was in store the next day.

That morning I walked to our shop. When I opened the door, I heard the sound of a powerful waterfall, and I could see water falling from the ceiling over the whole room. I immediately noticed that the nine-foot Steinway piano was ruined. My knees buckled and I almost fainted from the shock. Everything was soaked with water except the table holding our sacred objects. It had been mysteriously protected. When the outside water line was shut off, the insurance companies and local authorities began their investigations. To everyone's surprise, no one lived above the place and no water lines had leaked or been turned on from above. Both groups had to conclude that there was no natural explanation for the waterfall. The caretaker of the building noticed how our personal mojo was not touched, and this made him nervous. It was Hillary who then saw that a chicken foot with a colored ribbon wrapped around it was also sitting on the altar. We had not placed it there. Word immediately got out that a "voodoo" event had transpired at Chartres Street. The particular mojo item was fortunately not a curse, but a blessing—which made it all the more mysterious. The story has a happy ending. The insurance gave us full reimbursement for what had been damaged, including the purchase of any concert piano we desired. To folks from New Orleans, this result was not the usual outcome; insurance companies usually aren't generous after a calamity. Yet in our case, we ended up with the financial resources to start our work all over again.

Until we figured out where to go, we conducted numerous Sacred Ecstatics gatherings in a shotgun house in the French Quarter of New Orleans. We also conducted gatherings all over the world wherever we were invited to teach. Finally, we moved to Hollywood to be near our son, Scott, also known as DJ Skee. He was the host of a weekly television program near where we lived, and we attended and celebrated his professional life. We gave away all our furniture except for four chairs and a Steinway grand piano in order to squeeze into a small bungalow. Our bed actually hung from the ceiling and had to be pulled down every night. While southern California was the last place we ever imagined moving, we went to be near Scott and knew that we would always be led to wherever we needed to be. In spite of my aversion to New Age locales and the plastic nature of Hollywood, there we were in the middle of it all. In a tiny bungalow, mystery knocked on our door and again changed our lives.

Part Two

The Hollywood Visions

The Mystical Books of Life

The Hollywood visions began with nightly dreams of being in spirited ceremonies, Bushman dances, praise meetings, and other ecstatic gatherings. I'd wake up shaking and singing. Hillary soon started receiving songs in vision as well. Music filled our home and we were spiritually on fire.

One evening the nature of the dreams changed. Rather than being filled with song, I was sent to a visionary library where I was shown the source of wisdom that previous seers, such as Emmanuel Swedenborg, Rudolph Steiner, and Edgar Cayce, have tapped. I saw what has been variously called "Akasha," the "Akashic Records," or "The Book of Life." *Akasha* is a Hindu word meaning "sky," "space," or "ether," and its records reside in a nonphysical, mystical realm. H. P. Blavatsky referred to these records as "the indestructible tablets of the astral light."[17] The information found in these books, tablets, and records may appear in various forms. I have read texts, heard spoken words, seen light, witnessed music and dance, and experienced special emotion stored in a book-like container that is absorbed when the "book" is opened. Whatever form mystical knowledge takes, it is both held in and conveyed through vibration. The higher the vibration and the equivalent sympathetic resonance one has with it, the more wisdom can be imparted.

During this particular journey to the mystical library, I was shown how it operates and how it is organized. I also saw how others in the past had come to receive its holdings. One room contained the medical diagnostic knowledge that is stored in each person's energetic fingerprint. Another room concerned prophecy. When I entered it, three different books were held up in front of me. Each title specified something that would occur in the future. One book involved a discovery that will change our understanding of a major historical event from the past, another book was on a topic that could not be comprehended with our present level of knowledge, and the final book was about a scientific breakthrough that will follow the discovery of a unique "L-cluster" in the brain.

As I experienced all this news of the future, I felt uninspired. Though it was magical and incredible, it felt cold and lacked the fire of spiritual ecstasy. I said out loud, "I'd rather be deeply touched by prayer and song than open a file cabinet and retrieve another word."

I actually felt sorry for those former psychics and seers who were burdened with the task of going into trance to retrieve medical data or gather background information. They missed the super-charged ecstatic vibrations that automatically empower any subsequent healing, teaching, and transformative work done with others. Unfortunately, people are too easily distracted by the fantasy of channeling or tapping into other worldly data. They are unaware that information that feeds knowing is less valuable than songs that awaken higher emotion—the latter simply has more vibrational energy. Too many spiritual travellers are sidetracked searching through files within the mystical library and never arrive at the praise room, the concert hall, or the ceremonial dance floor. It is more rewarding and beneficial to go all the way to the upper room where the soulful music that imparts the highest vibrations is found.

Stay on the straight and narrow path to the divine, what we call the "vertical rope"[18] to God. If, along the way, you are meant to visit the mystical library to retrieve knowledge of some kind, then the divine will lead you there. However, this is not the ultimate destination of the spiritual journey; it is only a roadside stop. The library exists to provide infinite teachings that aim to help you and others go further in your spiritual traveling. When you are ready, you will be taken to the big upper room where the brightest light and greatest love reside, as well as the hottest divine fire that will set your soul ablaze.

The "Cutouts"

I dreamed of going to the library again and this time I met the neurophysiologist and cybernetician Warren McCulloch. He opened a book to show a particular page and then pointed to one circled name: William Burroughs. Through this Beat writer and poet I was introduced to a mystical teaching about the nature of trickster mind and how human beings use it to communicate. Specifically, I learned that the mind works in a way that is similar to the Dadaist cut-up technique for producing art. For example, a poem can be composed by randomly chopping up a text and then pasting the cutouts back together. The same technique can be applied to paintings and audio recordings. We didn't know anything about the history of this technique before the dream. We learned that poet Tristan Tzara used this method in the 1920s, creating a poem on the spot by randomly pulling words out of a hat. In the 1950s, painter and writer Brion Gysin rediscovered this method and introduced it to William Burroughs, who applied it to newspaper pages (something Tzara also did), cutting up linear sentences and then inventively splicing them together to generate a poem. Burroughs also did this kind of collage work with audio recordings. He bizarrely claimed to have discovered that it was a means of divination, saying, "when you cut into the present the future leaks out."[19]

In this visionary classroom I learned that when you are spiritually tuned, you readily notice the most important cutouts that take place in communication. This process requires that you avoid the conventional habits of listening and abandon the usual emphasis on trying to consciously "hear" and "understand" others. On the other hand, when you are out of tune, you typically give equal importance to everything said while searching for some underlying coherence (whether it is there or not). This gets you easily lost and makes it nearly impossible to discern the more resourceful, interesting, and vital cutouts that can help lift, ignite, and transform a situation.

It is fitting that it was the cybernetician Warren McCulloch (also a poet) who pointed me to William Burroughs. Hillary and I have dedicated considerable scholarship to arguing the cybernetic perspective that communication is a process of reality *construction*, not *reception*. Rather than "receive" someone else's intended meaning, it is more accurate to say that you boldly invent a meaning and reality out of something that is more noise than signal, more cutouts than a pattern that connects, more disconnected sound bites than a coherent story line. Listening to another person is a process of construing order out of disorder. You make meaning by selecting, slicing, trimming, fitting, and pasting another person's communication into your own frames of reference. When you assume that you can entirely suspend your active handiwork and sit back to listen more "openly," you are only imposing another cutout.

On the other hand, if you do something contrary to what you are taught to do in a conversation—avoid giving excessive attention to another person's talk, do not habitually construe meaning, do not aim to discover their[e] story, and do not assume you can ever understand them — that which is most important for fostering change will more likely be noticed. This radical approach runs contrary to popular assumptions about the nature of how we communicate with one another. Here, you not only regard another person's discourse as a stream of cutouts; you additionally regard your own thoughts and understandings about their talk to be little more than your cutting out *their* cutouts. Satirists are well known for cutting up politician's speeches and rearranging them to make what they say seem funny. This was the subject of a BBC radio documentary called *Cutting Up the Cut-Up*.[20] You, too, are always cutting up and cutting out the cutouts; all communication is a stream of ongoing cutouts where you make your own cutouts of other cutouts. What matters is *how* you cut things out and *how* you put them back together again; aim to cut into the present to construct a new and transformed future.

Keep your ears attuned to whatever stands out and is heard in spite of your effort not to hear anything. You may be familiar with this process naturally taking place when you suddenly hear parts of a conversation spoken by someone across a crowded room. When something important is said, you notice it, whereas before there was only background noise. Do the same when you listen to any person. Regard talk as mostly background noise and allow whatever is important to stand out on its own. The words and metaphors that serve transformation will then have a better chance of catching your attention. These cutouts are like the hidden markings of a scout or guide left to indicate a secret trail. Here, you attend to what is usually ignored and not noticed — the signs of a pathway elsewhere — while filtering out content that is more predictable, obvious, and trite.

---

[e] Here and throughout the book we often use "they" as a singular, gender-neutral pronoun.

When spiritually tuned you notice the cutouts that point to somewhere new and different by effectively listening via "not listening" to the words. Instead, you emphasize feeling the underlying vitality of what is spoken. The discernment offered by Sacred Ecstatics detects the cutouts of communication that pulse with life force. Rather than search for meaning, you hunt for the sacred vibration.[f] Once enough of these cutouts are gathered, the emphasis will not be on piecing them together to form another clichéd meaning, recycled interpretation, or typical story. Instead, your goal is to connect them in ways that further intensify and sustain the pulse of sacred vibration. This process requires a relationship with higher guidance, something only accomplished while standing in the big room of mystery. Allow higher hands to both make the cutouts and weave them together with sacred thread, constructing a different, transformed reality that is mystically charged.

Generating and reassembling cutouts is part of the natural process of creation. It is the means through which all things, including you and your experience, are created through differentiation from and reintegration with the ultimate indivisible whole of life. Construction, deconstruction, and reconstruction comprise the repeating cycle of life, death, and rebirth — the ongoing reincarnation of your everyday existence. Spiritually uncooked human beings generally can't tell the difference between a trivial and nontrivial cutout (one with or without the sacred vibration, respectively). Fortunately, there are higher hands that can help you sort it all out. You must learn how to "feel" the pull of the rope to God that discerns what is vitally important to notice in a stream of communication. With a

---

[f] We coined the term, "sacred vibration," to refer to the divine, creative life force that goes by many other names including *chi*, *n/om* (the Kalahari Bushmen), *seiki* (Japan), and holy spirit, among others. We discuss the sacred vibration in depth in our book, *Sacred Ecstatics: The Recipe for Setting Your Soul on Fire.*

divine hookup, you are rendered more able to discern the noteworthy elements that help awaken and electrify a radically transformed life.

The Singular Truth: God's Sweet Love

Last night I journeyed to a spiritual classroom where I was with Hillary and my mother, meeting my paternal grandmother's sister. My grandmother, Virginia A. Keeney, was a spiritual woman who lived to be in her nineties. As an elder she taught Sunday school to the adults at her country church. She had so much faith that when her husband, a devoted pastor, passed away she shed not a tear, saying he simply went ahead of her and is waiting for her to join him again in the future. My grandmother has appeared numerous times in my spiritual visions, as has my grandfather. This time Hillary and I met my grandmother's sister, Nell.

> In the vision, Nell held up a white tape recorder with glowing knobs. It was a luminous recording device. She looked at me and spoke into the microphone, saying, "I hereby testify that the love Brad speaks of is the pure and sweet love of God." She then made sure that her testimony had been successfully recorded. Pressing the luminous button one more time, she checked that the recorder was doing its job, and repeated the same words, saying that the love being discussed is "the pure and sweet love of God." Hillary and I then looked into her eyes and we began to weep as we felt God's sweet love pour into us.

I woke up praising the highest source from which all mystical blessings flow. At the end of each day and night, Hillary and I come home to a singular truth, the one supreme cutout of wisdom that should stand out above all else: God's love. Love God and be immersed in this love, making it the most important cutout in your life. Doing so will guide you to find and make other cutouts that help God's love spread and flourish.

Finding Ezekiel's Wheel

Years ago, on the first night of my arrival at the Caribbean island of St. Vincent, I had a dream of a red-carpeted staircase in the sky. I climbed it to find a shining gold throne, and there a voice spoke, "Archbishop Pompey has God's number." The next morning I asked my guide whether he had heard of a man with this name. He said that Archbishop Pompey was the head of the St. Vincent Shakers (also called Spiritual Baptists), and that he resided at the northern part of the island. We immediately took off on a journey to find him. Four hours later I shared my dream with the Archbishop and the old man authoritatively replied, "Yes, I do have God's number."

That night I again dreamed of the red carpet suspended in the evening sky. I woke up and got on my knees praying for direction. I was advised by my inner voice to go mourn and fast with Archbishop Pompey, and that I would receive further instruction and guidance. The next night I awakened to find my right arm lifted by some invisible hand and pulled off the bed—I was physically suspended over the mattress. I thought I'd be pulled all the way to the ceiling, but then I was dropped. Startled by this visionary levitation and suspension in the air, I wasted no time telling the Archbishop what had happened. He confirmed that this was very serious and that God was calling me to enter into more mystery.

I entered a weeklong fast under the Archbishop's supervision, prayed over by the community of Shakers.

> I had a vision in which I was lifted off the earth, this time taken high into the visionary clouds. There I met an ancient, white-bearded man who said, "I am Ezekiel and will be your teacher, guide, and pointer

(one who directs spiritual travel). You have entered my school, The Holy Ghost Tabernacle of the Four Directions. I will lead you to do everything four ways. I will teach you many things and you will ask me whatever you want to know. Rejoice in this."

Ezekiel discussed the wheel he had seen in his Biblical vision, explaining how the sacred wheel concerned the turning and churning of spiritual power. He first revealed it as a donut-like shape of foggy wind, saying that "the power of the Holy Ghost is a sacred wind sent down to open hearts, to fill them with energy and vision." As I heard the wheel's singing sound and felt its vibratory power, I saw the spiritual ropes[g] wrapped around its rim.

I was taken on numerous spiritual journeys with Ezekiel; they included going to Mt. Zion to receive my spiritual anointment and appointment. I later went inside a spiritual hospital and was operated on. I was also placed in the river Jordan and given its water to drink, as a paintbrush was dipped into the river and used to paint a blue cross on my back. In the Sinai wilderness I was shown the temptations of the world while a branding iron marked my hands and feet. Finally, I was sent to Calvary where I learned firsthand about the miraculous transformation of suffering into extreme heavenly joy.

During these visions, I was taught how Ezekiel's wheel can reveal the highest teachings, including God's number, but the wheel must be turned for its truth to be released. If the wheel is stopped, the truth of a teaching can die and even begin to perpetuate its opposite. For example, I have learned to ignore the false, frozen depiction of Jesus that hardened enthusiasts proclaim while voicing hatred of others. I only follow the loving

---

[g] A rope is also a highway for spiritual visionary travel.

Jesus who inspires forgiveness and sharing. The latter operates inside the turning, churning, and changing spiritual wheel, asserting a love so big it cannot be captured, stilled, or reduced by unchanging human law. Similarly, I avoid the false Buddha set forth by those whose overproliferation of word and thought tightens the yoke he wished to revoke. When the wheel of creation stops turning, any formerly true teaching becomes reversed, and its spiritual power dissipates. This is how it goes for all the great wisdom traditions—truths are made false, love converts into hatred, mystery hands itself over to the known, and energy becomes powerless whenever trickster takes the wheel and halts the movement of creation. In the turning, however, the changing truth of creation is infused into every wisdom teaching, rendering it ready for experiential absorption.

Receiving the Wheel

In Hollywood I had another encounter with the mystical wheel.

> I was taken to a kind of class reunion where I glimpsed my former teachers during an extremely fast mystical flight. Landing in a huge campus-like place, I held the brown and weathered leather briefcase I owned when I was nineteen years old, at the time of my first mystical illumination. It seemed I had been sent to a major spiritual university. After being interviewed by various faculty members who appeared to constitute an administrative committee, I opened the briefcase to find pages of notes from my previous spiritual journeys. There were also letters of recommendations from various teachers, including one that inspired an elder committee member to say, "This is most curious because this is the first letter of endorsement she has ever given," making reference to a particular woman teacher who was apparently

known for being quite rigorous, critical, and demanding.

After consulting with one another, the spiritual teachers asked me to follow them to a gigantic building. "Inside it," a voice said, "is the classroom where you will go do your work." I was struck by the realization that this was the first time I would not be a student in a spiritual classroom; I was being assigned a teaching position. I wondered whether I'd be sent to the Kalahari, Japan, Amazonia, Greenland, or elsewhere. To my surprise, they opened a door and there, suspended in space, sat what looked like a giant, luminous metallic object—a circular donut with four spokes. In its center was a room. The voice spoke again, "This is your classroom. It is Ezekiel's wheel."

I woke up trembling. I had again seen Ezekiel's wheel, this time solid and luminous, suspended in the air at a 45-degree angle with the lower right quadrant near the ground. I immediately recalled how this classroom was also a major portal to visionary places; it could transport you anywhere. I wondered to myself, "Why do my visions of Ezekiel's wheel only reveal one wheel when most people think it consists of four wheels?" I later found that Ezekiel's first impression in his vision was actually of "one wheel upon the earth" (Ezekiel 1:15);[21] it was only later that he changed his description to be that of four wheels (Ezekiel 10:9). The voice within me spoke: "There is only one wheel, but everything is held and manifest four ways." In the turning of this single wheel through four directions is found "the spiritual mystery and power" it embodies. I was stunned at how the pieces of a mystical puzzle were being brought together. Each vision was a divine cutout being put together by higher hands, piece by piece.

I learned what the Merkabah Jewish mystics taught: This

wheel is linked to the source of vision, spiritual teaching, and higher spiritual dimensions. In Biblical days, visionary journeys to the spiritual classrooms took place on a "chariot of fire" or "horse of fire." Similarly, God would visit prophets on a chariot of fire. The Hebrew word *merkabah* refers to both a chariot (or seat) to ride on as well as a heavenly throne and place for the divine. To ride the blazing chariot and get to the throne at the top of Jacob's ladder, one must endure a long odyssey that includes numerous existential death and resurrection experiences. Like the pilgrim in John Bunyan's book, *Pilgrim's Progress*[22] (the public library in St. Vincent catalogues this book as "nonfiction" for the way it accurately details many of their mystical teachings), I had to get a ticket and certificate that allowed admission to the Celestial City. Along the way, I met those who housed and protected me, faced a giant monster that tried to kill me, went to a desert-like valley where the shadow of death awaited, experienced the carnival of spiritual vanity with all its magic tricks, went past faith and talk, ignored the false prophet named "By-ends" who teaches that religion brings prosperity, marched past the Plain of Ease, the Doubting Castle with its Giant Despair, risked my life crossing the Error and Caution Mountains where shortcuts lead to perilous times, and then ignored Ignorance and Flatterer, before forcing myself to wake up in the Sleep-Inducing Enchanted Ground that is like the poppy fields described in the *Wizard of Oz* children's tale. Finally I stepped into the river without a bridge in Beulah Land for it was the final crossing before entering the gate to the Celestial City. As I stepped into the river, the power of divine love lifted me as I passed into glory.

Laying Down Spiritual Tracks for the Wheel

The next night I was taken back inside the wheel where a visionary voice provided instruction, "Take those who spiritually hunger to the classrooms. With an anointed voice, invite them to come along. Each telling of a visit to the classrooms helps lay down a track that others can later follow. Once a track is laid, the spiritual heat of vibration and song can turn the wheel of transport and travel upon its groove." In vision, Hillary and I were anointed to invite others to the visionary terminal of spiritual transportation, the starting point for spiritual journeying. We were also reminded that any detailed description of a vision matters less than whether your heart was warmed and sweetened by divine grace.

As Dante said, "As one who sees in dreams and wakes to find the emotional impression of his vision still powerful while its parts fade from his mind—Just such am I, having lost nearly all the vision itself, while in my heart I feel the sweetness of it yet distill and fall."[23]

Ezekiel's wheel enables travel to the spiritual classrooms. You spiritually journey to be in the midst of creation's changing, the process of creation itself. Wherever you are sent, you find that all mystical visions point you to the same essential teaching, though the forms in which the latter is conveyed are diverse and often shifting. Each journey takes you to the illumined truth concerning the vast mystery of divinity, a reconfirmation that God's love answers and conquers all. After a particular teaching is received and shared with the world, trickster eventually finds a way to distort and bend it, making the conveyance of holy wisdom more difficult. This is why another, different teaching is delivered to straighten the spiritual rope and keep you on the sacred road. There is no end to visionary teaching. In this changing, the divine rope remains fastened to holiness and conquers every trickster effort to bottle and diminish it.

Ezekiel's wheel may at any time transform into a train, a car, a ship, a chariot, a horse, a mule, a space capsule, an elevator, a bubble, or any form of transportation. It is sent to pick you up and carry you to the visionary classrooms. You can be taken many times and in various ways, or you may only be taken once. In general, do not trust any visionary travel that lacks spiritual heat[h] unless supervised by a spiritually cooked wisdom teacher. Otherwise, trickster will likely give you a ride to nowhere, even though it may seem at the time like you had a big vision. In the hotter spiritual temperatures, the journey crosses into the depths of your heart where you may be gifted with a key or a ticket to travel, accompanied by a mystical song. The most important mystical travel is heated by sacred song. All other dreaming and contrived spiritual journeying should be held suspect.

There are many references to the mystical wheel or chariot among the religions of the world. The hymns of the *Rig Veda* report that Indo-Aryan priests had visions of a chariot consisting of three wheels that can be bent by the minds of the priests.[24] The Aboriginal "Men of High Degree" enter the spirit world by constructing a set of concentric rings on the ground, a type of portal to move back and forth between the earth and the Dreamtime. Daoist Zhang Ling reports in *The Scripture of Great Peace* that "The splendor of *Yang* starts to shine and spread its light. . . . Its *chi* [energy] turns and circles like the wheels of a chariot."[25] The column of light through which Edgar Cayce spiritually traveled was wound around a wheel, "like the Rotarians have."[26] In *The Epitome of the Six Yogas*, Naropa, the Tantric Buddhist teacher, advised, "Meditate on 4 wheels."[27] Al-'Arabi said that he, like Mohammed, "was enveloped by lights until I became wholly light" which gave him "knowledge of 'entering and circularity,' . . . [and] this circularity is not a

---

[h] Here "spiritual heat" refers to the presence of strong heartfelt emotion, sacred vibration, and music in a vision. For more on the spiritual thermometer see Chapter 2 in our book, *Sacred Ecstatics: The Recipe for Setting Your Soul on Fire.*

matter of not doing, it is actually what is happening."[28] In *The Book of Life*, Beatrice of Nazareth, a Cistercian nun, found that "[a]s soon as she was raised aloft in ecstasy, she saw beneath her feet the whole world as if it were a wheel."[29]

The night after receiving Ezekiel's wheel at the spiritual university, I had another vision of it. This experience was so strong that I thought I was awake in the daytime.

> In the dream Hillary and I went outside, looked to the sky, and saw the sacred wheel. It was so extraordinarily beautiful and powerful that I trembled at the sight of it. The wheel hovered above the ground at a 45-degree angle and revealed that it was attached to a long tube that extended high into the sky. The wheel then lit up with a display of colors that were not actually colors, but some other kind of sensory experience beyond physical vision that I cannot describe. I was informed that there should be no doubt that this was Ezekiel's wheel. Then the rope whipped itself at the end and propelled the wheel into the sky beyond sight. After it disappeared, we went on with the day, but I could not get it out of my mind and kept talking about it. I said things like, "We saw it while we were wide awake and it was truly overwhelming," and "We must tell others that we saw it in the daytime sky."

I then woke up and was surprised to find that this entire experience, including when I thought I had awakened, had been held inside a vision. The dream felt more real than being awake.

Everyone Has a Luminous Egg

In a subsequent vision twenty-four hours later, I beheld a green valley filled with luminous ostrich eggs.

There were more eggs than I could see or count. I was shown that every human being is given a divine egg. You must spiritually warm the egg before you can hatch its gift and bring its special emotion to life. In the vision I heard, "Devotion awakens the emotion that carries you to the divine ocean of love." Whether the egg cracks open is between you and God. However, be assured that there is a divine egg nearby. It is glowing, radiating, and throwing out sunbeams, moonbeams, ecstatic rays, and luminous ropes to bring you closer to divinity. Step toward this mystery. You and this light have been waiting for one another.

In the beginning was the cosmic egg, faced in the holiest Bushman vision. The "egg-shaped cosmos," called *Brahmanda*, is found in Sanskrit scriptures. The Upanishads say that an egg, called *Hiranyagarbha*, floated around in emptiness until it broke into two halves that formed heaven and earth. The cosmic egg is the primary symbol for resurrection and rebirth. Hildegard's vision, known as "The Cosmic Egg," once again placed this image at the center of the spiritual cosmos. Various cultures all over the world have honored the ovum mysterium: witness the golden egg of the Hindu, the ancient Egyptian sun-egg, the Dogon egg of the creator-god, the cosmic, serpent-encircled egg of the Greek Orphic religion, or the Hopi Mystery Egg at the end of the current Fourth World.

Several weeks after I saw the green valley of eggs, Hillary was taken to a related spiritual classroom.

In the dream, Hillary's father led her to a gathering of people. When she arrived the elders reminded her that she had volunteered to help. They took her over to an area that was full of chickens walking freely on a green lawn. All around them were broken eggs; the yolk was seeping out and pooling everywhere in the grass. This was revolting to her and she was disgusted at having to walk through it, taking care to keep the mess off her feet. She felt nauseous and wanted to remove herself from the situation, but remembered she had made a pledge to be of service.

When Hillary woke up and told this dream to me, I told her that I had spent much of the night praying with agony about how difficult it is to bring authentic spiritual teaching into the world, when human beings often do not have the discipline, patience, humility, clarity, wisdom, and spiritual warmth to care for the egg and help it hatch. Instead, people try to force themselves through the shell, laying all to waste with careless ego striving. We become too eager for spiritual accomplishment and come out of the egg as a big, messy presence rather than a tiny newborn chick or child of God.

Hillary replied that she also had gone to sleep praying and lamenting the ways we all so easily get lost, aggrandizing the self rather than surrendering in our smallness to divine mystery. We do so even when we intend not to. We are always just a hairsbreadth from losing our compass and falling off the path.

The next morning after Hillary's vision, our dear friend Debra sent us an email:

Last night I had a dream. I knew I was in a hatchery and saw myself sprawled on my stomach on top of a very large white egg. My arms and legs were open and stretched out to have maximum contact with it. I felt like I had a responsibility to the egg that a mother hen would have to safeguard hers prior to hatching. I was "sitting" on it and I was very focused, comfortable, and confident. Without looking away from the egg, I was aware that Brad and some others were nearby on the left. Brad said to them, "She's ready. It can go into the world."

These visionary teachings address what is required for the hatching of the spiritual egg, and serve as reminders of how to nurture and bring life to the spiritual wisdom we are asked to mother. Our care and protection make it possible for spiritual truth to be birthed again. Notice these words or cutouts that stand out in Debra's vision: *maximum contact, focus,* and *not looking away.* Each of us has a spiritual ostrich egg from God that has the potential for hatching. It is so easy, however, to fail to do what is necessary to allow the egg to incubate and grow in a good way so that it may hatch. You must totally focus on God and not be distracted, doing so with maximum contact with the holy egg. You cannot force the egg to open; this only risks it breaking too early and letting the yolk seep out. Like a mother, you must patiently wait for the biggest mystery to be released in its natural time.

The Spiritual Password

The next night I received visionary guidance to do what I had never done before — I gave out a mystical password to the visionary spiritual classrooms, doing so for a whole group of mentorship students. A password is traditionally given by "spiritual pointers" of ecstatic lineages to take you to the starting point of a mystical journey. When people seek a vision by solo means, they almost always get distracted by trickster and end up chasing wishful fantasy. In long-lasting wisdom traditions, elders anointed to guide others in visionary travel help the seeker head toward the high roads. The password, dreamed by the pointer, helps keep the traveler pointed in the right direction.[30]

I gave such a password to our class of students and explained that they were supposed to focus on it without distraction. This password must be constantly spoken to oneself, even amidst prayer and song. It is like a mantra, a seed crystal, or a primary mystical cutout infused with intense spiritual power. As a compass it helps keep you near the vertical rope to the divine. If you catch yourself pondering what the words mean, inject more emotional intensity into your expression in order to reel yourself back from contemplative drift and any distraction generated by rambling internal commentary. The password is not only a focal point; it is your boarding ticket for a train bound for the big room of mystery.

The specific password was a phrase given to our class: "*All these things will I give you or Thou shall worship the Lord thy God.*" This password is the choice Jesus faced when he went into the Mt. Sinai wilderness and encountered temptation. Trickster promises you specific outcomes, powers, and delights, including the widest selection of spiritual experiences and achievements. When you ask for anything that has a specific name, trickster arrives to be of service. In vision, I was shown that the highest crossing at the spiritual crossroads requires that you forgo *asking* for anything and instead turn to *worshipping* the divine: "All these things will I give you or Thou shall worship the Lord thy God."

At some point every spiritual journey takes you to the crossroads where you face the ultimate choice. It is the devilish trickster of your consciously purposeful mind that confuses getting what you want with spiritual fulfillment. Contrary to what many have said and heard, God is not the head of a Sears and Roebuck spiritual mail-order company, but the host of the Infinite House of Holy Light, the mystery of which renders you speechless. Choose to worship before the ineffable. You may not receive what you initially think you desire, but you will be truly living in the biggest, holiest room. When we gave our class the spiritual password from Mt. Sinai, a number of students were taken to the crossroads in vision. They either came to the Grand Central Station of Ezekiel's wheel that was manifest in various forms (including an airport terminal) or they found themselves seeing or hearing mystery on the other side of a wall or mountain.

A password begins as a spiritual compass that points you in the right direction. If wholeheartedly held with sincere conviction and saturation, the password will start to chant and sing itself, delivering a sacred vibration. In the stormy sea, prayer fast, vision plea, and mourning ground, holy words of prayer are transformed into a song that is a lifeline to God. For the rest of your life, when trouble comes knocking on your door or suffering throws you down, you will reach for this song. Once a song is received and owned in this way, you know how to sing it so sincerely that it readily awakens and uncoils your rope to God. Through this divine hookup you are always pointed in the right direction and given all you need to stay on the path.

The Rope to God

I was once awakened in the middle of the night by a thunderous voice that announced, "I am the voice of God. I will show you my face." I had been taught in Sunday school that some Biblical characters had seen God in vision, but that it was not possible to see the face of divinity without perishing. Before I could think further, I was immediately transported in my vision to a high mountain in a fog or cloud of white light. I faced huge, pointed white masses of irregularly shaped, glacier-sized stones rising into the sky. The area was completely bathed in white light, making it impossible to clearly see. I was called to walk toward the edge near where divinity resided and as I did, the light became brighter, completely erasing any distinguishing features. The closer I came to the divine, the more its radiance overwhelmed my vision.

In 1976, I was hypnotized by a professor conducting research on altered states of consciousness. She asked me to re-experience my birth. I saw it taking place in an old propeller-driven airplane with a jagged hole in its side where people were lined up to jump out. When my turn came, I looked out the hole and saw many searchlights in the sky that were moving in different directions. It was a night sky filled with fog. In that moment I realized that the purpose of birth and of life itself was to concentrate in such a way that all these beams of light would align themselves as one light. This singular focus required unbending attention to the source of all light. I had to jump, following that straight line down to earth. I would later learn that this is the same luminous rope to God required for ascent into the sky village of heaven.

Years afterward, I found out more about the rope to God in an unexpected way. One evening after I sang my young son his bedtime songs, I prayed silently, "Dear God, please show your presence to Scott. He is so immersed in the world of Nike shoes, toy action figures, and video games that I want him to know you are there. Let him know about your presence." He did not know what I had prayed.

We went to bed, and six hours later I awakened to hear Scott shouting in his room. "Dad, Dad, get in here! Get in here! I think someone has broken into the house!" Alarmed, I ran to his room to find him sitting up in bed in a state of shock. "What happened, Scott?" I asked. He replied, "I am not sure. It was like a dream except it was real. I was running down a street and I saw a rope hanging from the sky. I floated all the way to heaven and met God who told me how everything works."

I was astonished. God had answered my prayer. My son had experienced a voyage to divine mystery. He was given a rope to God and followed it all the way to heaven. I told him that he was very lucky because this was a special gift. I knew I shouldn't ask him what he heard, but I couldn't help myself. I asked anyway.

Scott replied, "I'm too tired to talk now. I want to go back to sleep." We never talked about it the next day; this experience was not for words. All that matters is that the rope will forever live inside his heart and come to him whenever it is needed or sincerely called upon.

One of our mentorship graduates wrote to tell us a report about his young son. We share his story as an inspirational teaching for everyone:

> Tonight I visited my son at his mom's place around dinnertime. I asked him if he had any recent dreams and he replied that he doesn't dream. I asked again, hoping he'd remember a dream, but he made clear that he never dreams. However, then he told me, "For the past few nights a rope that was hollow came down from my ceiling and sucked me up a tube like a vacuum, taking me to an empty field where I was the only person there." I said that this is a great dream and I asked him to pray that the rope will get stronger and take him all the way to heaven. He replied, "Daddy, I'm not dreaming. The rope comes when I'm awake." Then he told me more about this open field. I asked if he had ever heard me talk about a rope or hollow tube and he said he hadn't heard anyone mention it.

This account reminded me of an amazing Brazilian healer, Otavia Pimentel, who lived to be one hundred years old. She once told me a story about her childhood. When she was a young girl, she started climbing a luminous visionary staircase that took her to an open field. One day, a horse arrived in the field and it took her on a ride. She said it was the most beautiful place she had ever been. There she was taught how to help others.[31]

The rope to God is vertical. If you find yourself facing a horizontal rope, hand it over to God rather than mess with it on your own. Don't get lost exploring the ropes that connect you to other people, animals, spirits, or places. Leave them alone unless you are granted permission to access them underneath the canopy and guidance of greater divine illumination. You should never carelessly assume that the latter is true, for trickster can too easily convince you that this is the case. It is wiser for you to simply leave those ropes alone. If you are curious about them or feel them pulling you, consider it a sign that you should *not* chase them. Once you have a strong enough rope to God, the other ropes are not tempting. Similarly, Saint Teresa of Avila warned of the pitfalls that come with having too much desire for visionary experience. Wishful thinking makes it difficult to distinguish visions that come directly from God versus those invented by the mind. As such, Saint Teresa advised against paying too much attention to meditative visions. If visions come directly from God, it is okay to ignore them, because if God delivers something you don't understand he will come back and make it clear.[32]

At the same time, be respectful that all ropes derive from the one singular rope to God. When you first peer into the spiritual sky, you may perceive what appear as many lines or searchlights. With strong spiritual acuity and focus, the differences realign, converging and merging into one light from God.

Climbing the Rope

One of my dearest friends and colleagues, Bill Sutherland, a Canadian physician whom I have known for many decades, went through a dark night of the soul as he readied himself for a deepened relationship with divinity. Near the end of this journey into the valley of despair, the yoke in which he had been imprisoned was released. He had a dream of going up the rope and having an ancestor tell him that he was finally free. Bill reported his dream as follows:

Lisa [my wife] and I traveled to meet Hillary and Brad at a house in the country, but when we arrived they weren't home. The house was empty and closed up. It was a lovely country home with a porch and mature trees. We waited and waited, but they never arrived. As I was standing in the yard, I noticed a single thread suspended in midair. It was thin like a spider web, but there was nothing above for it to be attached to; there was only blue sky. When I reached for it I rapidly began to ascend and the thread transformed into a thick cable. I was standing on top of it. About 30 feet or so above the ground I looked down at Lisa and said, "Hey, you've got to join me." The cord motioned back on itself to pick up Lisa. Together we were quickly shot up to the sky. The house below disappeared from view and once above the clouds, we came upon a mountain high in the sky. On its top was a small, wooden one-room shack. On our way up the mountain on the cable, we passed one person making the journey on a small burro. When we arrived at the top we found Hillary and she said, "Most people haven't arrived yet, they're late." At the table in the room Brad sat beside my maternal grandfather. There were two other people at the other end of the table that I did not recognize. Brad was smiling. My grandfather looked at me and said, "I am glad you are finally out of jail."

In this dream, Bill was set free in a high spiritual classroom. He first had to find the thread, string, or rope before he could ascend. You are lost until you find the divine main line. Once you step toward it, you go up with ease and find yourself welcomed among family, teachers, and friends; you will be renewed and made ready to begin all over again.

Release the Water and Hold Onto a Prayer Rope

In a vision, Hillary and I were in a one-room Cajun style cabin with a wise older woman whose face we could not see clearly. She said, "When it is time, I will open the gate of the dam and release the water." I looked out a window and saw a beautiful body of water, noticing that the cabin was high above it. I then turned and saw a shelf holding large jars of herbs and potions. The center jar had a label whose first word was "Bayou." A voice then said, "This is Washington."

The next morning I discovered that Washington, Louisiana is in the heart of Cajun country and that its bayous have supported various healers over the years. I also learned that a Catholic lay priest named "Father Mac" had arrived there years ago from Little Rock, Arkansas. His visions of the Virgin Mary and Jesus led to spontaneous healing abilities, and he received specific visionary instruction to prepare a holy "armada," a nautical metaphor for a fleet of spiritual ships. In his vision, each vessel is someone dedicated in prayer and devotion to God. He claimed that a new outpouring of the spirit would begin in Washington, Louisiana and other regions of the world. His teaching encourages praying the Rosary with an added beginning, requesting exceptional devotion—like spiritual armor—to help protect one from being led astray by any distraction. His congregation has reported apparitions of the Holy Mother and witnessed miracles. When I made contact with Father Mac and shared my visionary experience, he rejoiced and said, "We are being shown similar teaching and it is from heaven, straight from God."

Whereas a spiritual password helps keep you focused on a single spiritual cornerstone, the Rosary guides you along a path paved with prayer. Its sequence of prayers constructs a road to

God.[i] For prayer ropes and beads to work effectively, you must be wholeheartedly focused and spiritually heat your words through an infusion of sincere and intense emotion. The world's religions offer prayers as sacred tracks on which to move toward divine mystery. Hold a prayer string, voice its prayers, and let the motion of sacred emotion carry you forward. With Buddhist and Hindu prayer beads (*malas*), the Catholic Rosary, or Native American prayer ties and flags, you hold a physical string that in prayer becomes intertwined with the rope to God.

The Aural Sacramental Bridge of Franz Liszt

God's love is expressed through music, and those who bring down the songs are the shamans and mystics among us. I had a vision of seeing a cornerstone in Budapest with the name "Franz Liszt" and the year "1860" marked underneath it. I discovered that the composer had written a will that year, confessing that all his music issued from a "burning and mysterious feeling which has marked my whole life as with a sacred stigma. Yes, the crucified Jesus, the ardent yearning for the Cross and the exaltation of the Holy Cross, this was my true vocation."[33]

Franz Liszt was known for the ecstatic fervor of his performances. The "burning and mysterious feeling" he had within was somehow transformed and conveyed to his audience when he performed his music. People experienced emotional

---

[i] The introduction of a string of beads to count a sequence of prayers was introduced in the third century BCE in India while the Christian Desert Fathers used knotted prayer ropes during the same time in history. These prayer ropes are still a part of the habit of Eastern Orthodox monks and nuns. The Catholic Rosary is generally regarded as given to Saint Dominic in a Marian apparition that took place in 1214. Over the years, different saints and church leaders have sometimes modified the words, understandings, and practices that go along with it. What remains consistent is that it is held as a reminder to keep focused on moving through a progression of prayers, keeping the prayerful on the right track to holiness.

ecstasy or "Lisztomania," as it was called. Consider this early review of a Liszt concert written by Heinrich Heine:

> And what tremendous rejoicing and applause! — a delirium unparalleled. . . . The electric action of a demoniac nature . . . perhaps a magnetism in music itself, which is a spiritual malady which vibrates in most of us — all these phenomena never struck me so significantly or so painfully as in this concert of Liszt's.[34]

Liszt had a musical bridge to the divine, enabling its electricity, magnetism, and vibration to be delivered through the passage of music from heaven to earth. Though the resulting ecstasy was often demonized or pathologized by naïve observers, mature ecstatics of other cultural traditions would have recognized a kindred spirit in a man whose musical soul was on fire.

Franz Liszt regarded music as an "aural sacrament" that serves as a bridge between heaven and earth. Here music becomes a theophany of divine manifestation; that is to say, God is physically experienced when music imparts the sacred power of its divine source. Mind alone does not have the capacity to host or express the numinous blaze. It is music that carries the divine flame. Liszt touched upon the core of mystical and shamanic activity when he wrote, "Only in music does *feeling*, in manifesting itself, dispense with the help of reason and its means of expression, so inadequate in comparison . . ."[35] (emphasis ours). You journey to the mystery of divinity through what you feel in the most emotionally touching music, something that the thoughts of mind and reason cannot produce. Liszt's musical mysticism embraced this wisdom, which can be heard singing inside his question, "Is not music the mysterious language of a faraway spirit world whose wondrous accents, echoing within us, awaken us to a higher, more intensive life?"[36] This is the central truth of every genuine mystic and shaman whose gift of song enables journeying to the spirit lands.

Paul Barnes points out that the incarnational spirituality of Liszt is "nothing less than the visceral, physical encounter of God."[37] Only music is capable of emotionally and viscerally connecting you with the theophanies of higher mystery. The aural sacramental bridge is the rope to God. Without a sacred song to climb, the mystic, shaman, or saint cannot journey to the heavens. Without music, one remains an outside observer of the sacred rather than a full-bodied participant. The question that matters more than any question in spirituality, no matter the hosting religion, is whether you aim to look or to cook. Again, the latter requires a traveling song that takes you into the divine flame.

As Liszt wrote in the preface to his musical composition for the seven sacraments: "I intended to give expression to the feeling by which the Christian takes part in the mercy that lifts him out of earthly life and makes him aspire to the divine atmosphere of heaven."[38] This late work of Liszt expanded the ground for the later contributions of Scriabin's music of divine ecstasy as well as the mystical work of Satie, Schoenberg, and Stravinsky, among others. "Sumptuous tonal chords," including those found in the vast realm of dissonance and atonality, can reveal mystical illuminations and pulses as the changing action of creation brushes upon whatever chaos it happens to meet.[39] For Liszt, however, the journey aimed to bring him to the source of the burning within—the musical stigmata that marked his life, his compositions, and his audiences.

I dreamed of Liszt's cornerstone while in Budapest, and this inspired Hillary and me to visit the Liszt Museum at the Academy of Music, where his apartment is preserved as it was during his final years. There is found Liszt's personal icon of Christ, crucifix, and rosary with which he made his evening prayers. As I stood on the wooden floor where he had walked in his former home, grasping the crucifix he held while praying, my heart felt the undeniable truth that music is the sacred bridge between God and the human soul. It is the mystical bridge, the shamanic journey, the Bushman rope to God, and the eternal return to our ancestral home. Music is simply earth as it is in heaven.

Hillary Goes Under the Water and Receives Her Singing Voice

Hillary and I were conducting a Sacred Ecstatics intensive in Brazil, where for the first time she received the anointment to sing. As she tells the story in our book, *Sacred Ecstatics*:

> Brad had been chanting and shouting while accompanied by a professional drummer. The rhythms were slow and soulful, and the room was charged with spiritual electricity. Our Brazilian friends were trembling, shaking, and rocking in their seats. I suddenly felt a surge of energy rise up inside me. It came up into my throat and filled me with an overwhelming urge to open my voice and sing. I had never before experienced anything like it, yet the feeling was so natural I readily surrendered to it and spontaneously burst into improvised song. It was the first time I had ever sung in public. Normally I am not able to do more than carry a simple tune, but that morning the songs flowed from my heart so effortlessly that I was astonished by the sound of my own voice. It was as if songs were brought out of my voice by a mysterious force outside my control. It filled me with exhilarating bliss.[40]

The night before this took place Hillary had a vision:

> I dreamed that Brad and I were lying next to each other and he took hold of my hand. The ground underneath us disappeared and became a large body

of water. Without fear we sank into the water and found we could breathe while submerged. Brad drew me further down underneath until we came to a special place. Without saying anything, he proceeded to transmit the sacred vibration into my whole body. I felt strong energy pulse through my body that was unlike anything I had ever felt. I woke up shaking and filled with joy.

What Hillary didn't know at the time is that being submerged under water is one of the important spiritual journeys known among the St. Vincent Shakers. Sometimes mystical travelers are gifted with spiritual weights to help them sink all the way to the bottom of the spiritual sea, doing so without fear. Each step of your sinking or falling will paradoxically result in a corresponding step of spiritual rising. As you come closer to the infinite, know that you have been made more ready to go even deeper and higher into mystery.

Beethoven's Sacred Law

On January 27, 2015, I did something I had only done once before in my life — I prayed that Hillary be sent to the highest classrooms. I did this many years earlier for my son and that same night he went up the rope to God. While Hillary had visited numerous visionary classrooms before, this evening I prayed that she encounter the highest mysteries. I did not tell her that I made this prayer.

Hillary woke me up just after five in the morning, saying she had been sent to a spiritual classroom. She was overcome with emotion. After weeping together with joy, I asked her to immediately get up and write it down. Here is her report:

I was in a small classroom on an old campus. It seemed crowded even though there were less than ten students. It looked like the private school I attended as a teenager — a very traditional place with brick walls covered with ivy. I was very excited to be back in school because the teacher was challenging and I loved learning and being a good student. I sat at the front of the class and the teacher was stern.

The subject of the lesson was Ludwig van Beethoven. The instructor was teaching that Beethoven was not only a great composer, but also a scientist who discovered a very important equation. He found that when something is being measured, at some point it becomes its negative or opposite. For example, at a certain point, "+1" becomes "-1." Beethoven, the teacher said, first discovered this equation and scientific law in relationship to measuring a mountain. I was concentrating very hard and was excited for the teacher to reveal more about what seemed like an impossible theory to grasp fully, knowing that it held an important truth about the nature of reality.

As the teacher was slowly revealing more, I suddenly thought that time must be the missing factor. I raised my hand and asked, being deliberate and careful with my words, "But at what point in time — or at what *instance* — does the mountain become its negative?" I had an image in my mind of the fabric of time bending the mountain in on itself, and thought this surely must be what Beethoven had discovered. The teacher responded strictly, "Wait, we haven't gotten that far yet."

Then the teacher went on to say that Beethoven had been persecuted for being misunderstood and thrown in jail. There he languished, was forgotten by his peers, and almost lost his mind. He thought he could not finish developing his theory of how things can exist as both their positive and negative. He was utterly broken and felt he could no longer compose music. Afterward, the teacher said, after being released from jail, Beethoven sat alone one night in deep sorrow. At this moment in my vision I could actually see Beethoven slumped over in his chair, cast in darkness and shadow. It is difficult to convey the depth of sorrow and anguish I witnessed in him. Suddenly, however, I heard musical notes rise up and out of Beethoven's heart.

When I heard this, it pierced my heart and I began to weep. The teacher then went over to his piano and played the first few notes of the song that rose from Beethoven's heart, which I now recognized as the melody from "The Windmills of Your Mind." While this song was actually composed by Michel Legrand, it follows a similar harmonic progression that Beethoven used in "Moonlight Sonata." I felt the notes so deeply that I experienced myself merge with Beethoven—I could see inside Beethoven's heart and feel his sadness lift with every musical note. I exclaimed to the teacher, "This story and this music move me so much!" The teacher was very excited and I was surprised to notice that I was the only student in the class who was moved by the teaching.

Then the teacher said, "When Beethoven heard these notes arise from inside his heart, he immediately realized that the rest of his theory concerning the relationship of the positive and negative addressed the tension that enables the heart to open like an envelope, revealing musical notes that arise from empty space." I saw, floating in front of me, a small, white envelope shaped not like a letter envelope but like a pouch that opens at the top when the sides are squeezed slightly together. I understood that the music rose out of this space in Beethoven's heart. I was so moved by the truth of Beethoven's experience—that he was alone, broken, and nearly empty inside, and then the melody came bubbling up out of his heart and brought all of his life to fruition.

After telling me about the envelope, the teacher went back to his piano and played the entire song, "Windmills of Your Mind," in a classical style with such passion, precision, and fervor that I began weeping again. Words cannot readily convey the extraordinary emotion I felt. The music filled the room and I was saturated with the power of the song. Though this vision brought many teachings, its clearest teaching echoed what Brad had often told me: Music is the holiest medicine and a spiritual lifeline delivered straight from God into your heart. When all else fails and you are truly broken, divine music arrives to lift you straight to heaven.

We later discovered that Beethoven had written, "Music is the one incorporeal entrance into the higher world of knowledge which comprehends mankind but which mankind cannot comprehend."[41] Furthermore, he said, "Whoever gets to know and understand my music, will be freed from all the misery that drags down others."[42]

In an essay entitled "The Secret of Ludwig van Beethoven," written by LaRouche, Jr., the author proposes that Beethoven had a great scientific mind. He was able to keep it absorbed in concentration upon the creative act of composition by focusing on positive moods evoked by great inspiration, while at the same time feeling the negative moods of anger and upset incited by the "evil and stupidity" he encountered in his own life. In this holding of both the negative and positive sources of inspiration, he could achieve a musical composition that did not arrive at a final resolution, but was a unique kind of ongoing, generative form. LaRouche writes:

> The truth within such a Beethoven composition is not that it arrives through development at a final resolution, but that in its resolution it looks back upon the process by which this progress was realized. Hence, both in musical and in epistemological principle, the key to the *generative idea* of (especially) a late-Beethoven composition is those phrases which perform the revised function of a *stretto*. [43]

The "stretto" in a fugue is "the imitation of the subject in close succession, so that the answer enters before the subject is completed."[44] The melody is called to start again with another voice before the preceding voice has completed. In other words, there is a superimposition of the musical subject upon itself so that it moves forward contrapuntally. Here the ongoing re-entry of the music into the music is simultaneously a means of leading, accompanying, interacting with, and moving each voiced line, making the music a unique kind of whole that is constantly re-creating itself with circular reentry as it moves through time.

What listeners find in Beethoven's work is the surprise that takes place when the beginning and end fold back upon one another. Rather than a straight-line march to the fulfillment of an anticipated outcome, things turn around and become their opposites, constantly changing valence (positive to negative and vice versa) as the measures of music are performed, returned, imposed, juxtaposed, and composed.

The negative forces in Beethoven's life were not limited to his being misunderstood and misheard by others. They also included the great suffering brought by his deafness, a description of which can be found in his letters. His hearing loss made him more physically reliant upon finding the positive force of music through somatically felt vibration. It has been said that in his later years Beethoven removed the legs from his piano so he could feel the vibrations in the floor when he played. This is how he discovered that music and its composition are governed by the interaction of vibrations, whether experienced as movement in one's skin or the tympanic membrane of the ear. These laws of vibration govern the nature of mystical experience as well. Canudo, in his "Eloge de Beethoven," claims:

> In Beethoven, matter makes that effort to vibrate in light that enchanted the paradisal dream of Dante, absorbed in his God: the state that Christians symbolically call Paradise. . . . Music represents the maximum of vibrations in matter before it turns into light. . . . As matter in vibration, it masks the last limit between thought and fire. . . . In the hierarchy of "densities" of matter, it represents the beginning of fire, just as the sentiment that follows sensation represents the beginning of thought. Beethoven subtilized in it a thousand confused essences of nature, to which he gave a rhythm, an unbending Law, so that men might recognize them. He was the first to fix this Law, which in fact men had always glimpsed and which Bach had almost determined in the immense theistical shouts of his Cantatas, and above all in his Fugues.[45]

Beethoven's reliance upon vibration over sound led him to the handling of implicit laws concerning how vibration leads to the mystical sounds of music that human ears do not hear. As has been postulated, he heard his Ninth Symphony while deaf. Consider this letter written on February 1, 1924, sent to the New York Symphony Orchestra after they'd performed Beethoven's Ninth Symphony at Carnegie Hall. The writer said she could neither hear nor see but had placed her hand on the radio speaker. She wrote:

> What was my amazement to discover that I could feel, not only the vibrations, but also the impassioned rhythm, the throb and the urge of the music! . . . I could actually distinguish the cornets, the roll of the drums, deep-toned violas and violins singing in exquisite unison. . . . The great chorus throbbed against my fingers with poignant pause and flow. Then all the instruments and voices together burst forth—an ocean of heavenly vibration—and died away like winds when the atom is spent, ending in a delicate shower of sweet notes. . . .
>
> I could not help remembering that the great composer who poured forth such a flood of sweetness into the world was deaf like myself. I marveled at the power of his quenchless spirit by which out of his pain he wrought such joy for others. . . .
>
> Let me thank you warmly for all the delight which your beautiful music has brought to my household and to me.
>
> With kindest regards and best wishes, I am,
> Sincerely yours,
>
> Helen Keller[46]

Pierre Beaudry concludes:

> Beethoven had no choice but to settle his account with the domain of sense perception and consecrate the rest of his life to the domain of sublime universal ideas of principle. It was not an easy decision to make. As his so-called *Heiligenstadt Testament* of 1802, attests, the year when he composed this *Sonata in C-sharp minor* was THE turning point in his life, because

he knew he was becoming completely deaf. Again, the singularity, better still the paradox, was the absolute tension between something that was inevitable and the relentless urge to obey his destiny.[47]

Beethoven wrote in his own testament:

> But what a humiliation for me when someone standing next to me heard a flute in the distance and I heard nothing, or someone heard a shepherd singing and again, I heard nothing. Such incidents drove me almost to despair, a little more of that and I would have ended my life — it was only my art that held me back. Ah, it seemed to me impossible to leave the world until I had brought forth all that I felt was within me. So, I endured this wretched existence. . . . Divine One, thou seest my inmost soul, thou knowest that therein dwells the love of mankind and the desire to do good. —Oh fellow men, when at some point you read this, consider that you have done me an injustice; someone who has had misfortune may console himself to find a similar case to this, who despite all the limitations of Nature, nevertheless, did everything within his power to become accepted among worthy artists and men.[48]

Filled with despair at his own auditory deafness, disturbed by the spiritual deafness and arrogant ignorance of others who could neither hear nor feel what was essential about his music, and inspired by the quest that enables music to promote vibratory closeness to divinity, Beethoven arguably found the same general law of spirituality that had been practiced by Bushman dancers singing in the Kalahari for thousands of years. From inside the deepest longing and yearning of the heart arise the musical notes whose sacred vibration helps you climb the rope, lifting one toward the ultimate joy that is found amidst the utmost suffering. Words cannot reach this experience of simultaneous ecstasy and tragedy; it can only be felt and expressed through music.

Being Contrite of Spirit: "Are You Broken Yet?"

Several days after the vision of Beethoven, Hillary went to another spiritual classroom; there she met Mother Ralph from the St. Vincent Shakers, who was holding a Bible. In the dream, Hillary sent me a text message that she was with Mother Ralph. As Hillary dreamed this, I was also in a classroom, hearing someone speak these words while showing me a holy book: "To him . . . that trembles, can my word be read." In addition were these words from Isaiah 66:2: "'For My hand made all these things, Thus all these things came into being,' declares the LORD. 'But to this one I will look, To him who is humble and contrite of spirit, and who trembles at My word.'"

The biblical scholar John Gill elucidates that the phrase, "contrite of spirit" refers to "hard hearts being broken by the Spirit and word of God, and melted by the love and grace of God."[49] Here contrite means "smitten," "broken," and "crushed." Like Beethoven and all the saints and mystics, your heart must be broken in order to receive the sacred vibration, enabling God's trembling grace and love to reside within.

Later that same night I went to another spiritual classroom where I was taught that the first question to ask someone coming for spiritual healing or teaching should be, "Are you broken yet?" Holy ones throughout the ages have known that without brokenness there is no spiritual entry into the divine mysteries. Whether it is the experienced dismemberment of a shaman in the making or the sincere brokenheartedness and despair of a dedicated spiritual seeker who longs for divine encounter, human beings are only radically changed through a process that involves being taken to a dead end where all that is left is a pile of cutouts. You must first face your broken nature and abandon faith in how you formerly pasted your life together. Whether this process takes place in a vision fast or in the illumination of a clearly examined life review, the final conclusion is the same: miraculously putting the fragmented pieces of your life back together requires higher hands.

Here you find the hidden blessing inside the lives of those who have fallen into grievous error, mistake, sin, or personal tragedy. These people may have fewer doubts about their brokenness and be more ready to ask for a higher helping hand. Every human being, however, has arguably fallen enough to feel broken. What stops you from discerning this basic fact is your trickster mind that can put any gloss or spin on the situation. Listen to the yearning and longing of your heart and pay less attention to the excuses, rationalizations, and persuasive cons of your conscious mind. Be careful of masking this deep existential truth through the mindless repetition of platitudes and positive affirmations. Your life cannot be solved or resolved by mental trickery. You can only find peace and joy through facing your need for ongoing divine intervention.

Saints and mystics often regarded their inadequacy and weakness as a resource for their spiritual lives. After receiving a vision or an anointment, you are not made perfect, enlightened, or liberated from weakness and suffering. Instead, you discover how to use these qualities as spiritual gifts, and allow your weakness to help strengthen your rope to God.

Receiving the High Mark

As I pondered how brokenness and suffering are inseparable from spiritual transformation, I made this plea: "Oh Lord, I shall always be broken and in need of direction. I cannot make a single choice without you. I ask that you direct me over and over again as I shall forever hand my life over to you." I fell asleep and was soon sent to another spiritual classroom.

> There I was handed a small electronic screen about
> the size of a cell phone. A voice said, "This is from
> your Grandmother." The screen had a looped
> message, like a news crawl at the bottom of a
> television screen. It ended with this repeating phrase,
> "God has put a mark high on you."

I was so startled that I immediately woke up, and in a daze I remembered that there was a scripture about those who had been marked by God. My grandmother had reminded me that this mark is what everyone should seek. The mark or seal of God on a person indicates that the holy spirit resides within, and that the divine mission intended for one's life will be fulfilled.

When you surrender your brokenness to God's hands, you are remade in the spirit and a mark is placed high on your face, usually directly on the forehead. Being spiritually cooked makes and marks you as a vessel that is guided and pulled by a rope to God. As my grandmother would say, quoting Scripture, "This sets his seal of ownership on us, and put his Spirit in our hearts as a deposit, guaranteeing what is to come" (2 Corinthians 1:22). She would add that the angels have marked and sealed the foreheads of "the servants of our God" (Revelation 7:3).

You must keep moving forward along the straight and narrow road to God, walking across the incarnational bridge, aural rope, and mystical highway between flesh and spirit, the human condition and the kingdom of heaven, temporal suffering and eternal joy. Be careful whenever anyone asks the question, "Have you realized your perfection yet?" When you exalt the self as the host of the Godhead, you are led more deeply into the erroneous assumption that you, as a part of creation, constitute the whole of divine creation itself.

The other question—"Are you broken yet?"—points to your suffering and partiality that is in need of being resituated inside the divine whole. This is the highest prize: living inside the heart of God's love. Turn away from any temptation to exalt humanity over divinity, and yet do not regard them as dichotomous. Your place in the scheme of things is to reside within divine mystery. To receive the mark from God, you must be broken and shattered by the mighty wisdom sword, turned into holy cutouts, and then made whole again by the Big Holy. All else falls short of the mark. Allow God to make you a signed masterpiece, a broken piece made whole by the master.

Coronado

The cybernetic anthropologist Gregory Bateson once told me that the old debate over whether human beings are agents of free will or are subjects of determinism is resolved by the conclusion that one only has choice at the level of context. Once one steps into the chosen context, it determines the choices within. Translated into spiritual terms, this means the most important choice you have is whether you will reside in the infinite big room of the divine or a small room where there is only enough space for a self-shelf.

We arguably live in one of the most mixed-up times in human history, where a part (the self) is inflated and then incorrectly regarded as the whole (divinity). Whereas the New Age and New Thought masses claim that consciousness is evolving, a closer look reveals that we are more likely in a devolution rather than an evolution of spiritual know-how concerning how to nurture a strong relationship to the divine. Practically everything in the world now serves lowest-common-denominator outcomes: social popularity, enhanced finances, ideal body type, accumulation of materials, minimization of pain, maximization of comfort, and super-sized selfdom. This fantasized lifestyle glosses today's industries of entertainment, education, therapeutic practice, and spirituality.

In a dream, I heard a voice shout the name: "Coronado!" I

then saw the spiritual conquistadors of our time as those who have pillaged and appropriated the world's wisdom traditions, only bringing back extracted parts claimed to be magical, while leaving the greater whole context behind. What makes all forms of spirituality authentic, vibrant, and alive is that they serve (w)holiness rather than partialness. Unfortunately, trickster is arguably close to a complete takeover because it has successfully managed to cultivate a market for fake spiritual magic and neatly packaged pseudo-wisdom. In this dream, I heard trickster, the ultimate spiritual conquistador, speak to our time:

> *I offer all desired outcomes, including the new truth that your prosperity and abundance are part of the universe's luxury plan for your ultimate comfort. Only limiting beliefs and thoughts stand in the way of your commanding all the energies of the universe to manifest your personal will. The other choice – to get on your knees, be contrite of spirit, embrace your smallness, de-elevate the self, and value the way suffering can bring you closer to a heart full of joy – is a thing of the past. You have evolved past all that negativity and only need to focus on the positive. Ignore the teachings of all the ancient medicine people, saints, shamans, and healers who try to make you feel small. Instead, fatten your bank account with the power of now. Don't forget to say that it's not all about money because that also helps the money flow.*
>
> *Roll over Beethoven; I offer the most entertaining sound bites, infomercials, and Muzak piped into massage rooms across the country. Come on board the bullet train to self-glorification. Let's comfortably zoom along the fast track to success. Don't be distracted by any talk about going to the mourning ground or humbling yourself before God; that is only a bummer energy drain that ignores all the synergy you manifest whenever you think you are the*

best. Disregard Beethoven's embrace of both the negative and positive as a means of finding the ode to joy. Ignore the aural sacrament of Franz Liszt and instead compose your own wish list. Most importantly, why waste your time on prayer when you can think your way to being a millionaire?

Let me introduce you to the new marketplace where I have washed away the religions that bother, irritate, depress, disturb, and anger the self. Welcome to a life free of any request to sharpen your mind to handle confounding paradox and complex absurdity. It is better to repeat the simple mantras that assure your evolution of self to selfie, casting God in your own image. Would you like to harness the spirit without paying any dues or going through any ordeals? I have rendered and tendered all mysticism, healing, shamanism, and sainthood readily available and easily accessible (at the right price). Simply dial your desire and forget walking through any fabled sacred fire. It's better to take a pill and chill because God is a molecule ready to give a thrill. If you'd rather not ingest, may we suggest the new God helmet that is wired to give you a jolly jolt? Since it's all in your head, why tread the narrow road when you can forgo prayer to sit in your easy chair? Your true destiny is manifestery rather than mystery. Be a spiritually evolved conquistador and make claim to anything you want! Long live the spirit of Coronado!

The law of attraction is all you need, but pledge to never question whether it's all about greed. Blessed are the strong and proud of spirit, for they shall inherit the earth. Be as large as a camel for there is no longer an eye of the needle, crossroads, or gateless gate to pass through. Forget about having to spiritually die; go after the sugar pie in the consumer sky. Understanding physics is difficult, but reading Deepak Chopra's quantum pabulum will make you *feel smart and ready to put the cash cart before the dedicated spiritual workhorse. Come along and let's make you a hell of a deal that guarantees instant heaven. Pick a card, any card because this stacked deck assures you will avoid existential wreck. It's time to attract the second coming of the newborn dumbing and numbing that eliminates facing the truth of any shortcoming. May your self-governed will be done! In the name of yourself, feel free to mindfully proclaim from the center of your YOU-niverse, "Me-alujah!"*

Because life is often challenging, it is easy to be seduced by promises of quick access to success, happiness, health, and wealth. Likewise, spiritual hucksters are ready to satiate your longing for the divine by promising you full shamanic powers and healing mastery through simple-to-learn techniques. Whether it's sonic entrainment, body posture, hyperventilation, contacting spirit animals, or meditation and yoga without religion. We invite you to take another look at the wisdom lineages from which the parts that please trickster have been extracted and abstracted. Question whether these parts become impotent without the whole matrix from which they were born and made alive.

Trickster suggests on every front that you can have all the benefits of the whole by only dealing with the parts you like. We suggest that you consider the consequence of going for the core reductions and seductions rather than the whole complexity of indivisible holiness. The side(way) effects of that approach are often spiritually lethal. The choice at the crossroads between getting what you think you want versus handing your life over to the divine has always been the same, and it is as true today as it was in the past. The only thing new in the New Age is the new way it repackages the oldest temptation. Trickster has simply become trickier in finding ways to dupe you, now claiming that serving self and serving God are the same, and that being weak and meek are cause for shame.

Do you choose the lineage of the Mt. Sinai salesman who never stops trying to make a deal, or will you follow in the footsteps of those who are spiritually cooked? The real secret is that you have a bigger choice than what trickster offers. You have a choice to live in trickster's trinket mall or in the infinite divine universe.

Do not wake up in the morning and ask whether your body feels good and your mind feels at peace. That's living inside the smallness of self. You're likewise caught in that same smallness when you propose, "I think I'll try out God," and then the next day make a self-assessment to evaluate whether the god pill worked as well as an aspirin, a glass of carrot juice, a massage, or a yoga workout. The same is true of any spiritual practice: asking whether your prayers, meditation session, yoga posture, or shaking medicine dance are working or make you feel better the next day is nothing more than a sign that these things serve to please you rather than releasing you to please your maker.

A friend of ours who spent a life meditating and seeking spiritual growth and enlightenment from many teachers all over the world told us of an important spiritual lesson he received in a most unexpected way. He went on a diet that avoided all sugar. He was dedicated to this regimen and it was a part of his sincere motivation to become spiritually awakened. Then one night he had a vision. In his dream an old woman came to him and said, "Drink this and you will be enlightened." She handed him a glass filled with green liquid. The man paused and asked, "Does it have any sugar in it?" At that moment the woman shook her head and mumbled, "You are not ready for it." She withdrew the glass. He later regretted that his attachment to his ideas of good and bad short-circuited his reception of a mystical offering. We celebrated, however, that in denying him the glass of enlightenment a profound enlightened teaching was in fact delivered. This story is a reminder to all of us to put our trust in the greater wisdom mind of mystery rather than in our limited human preference and understanding.

Choosing to live in the vast whole universe means waking up in the morning and saying, "Thank you for another day of life." This gratitude is expressed and felt in a whole and holy way no matter what any particular part of your body or mind might feel or think. Say this sentence whether you are in a prison cell, hospital room, tipi, hogan, yurt, hut, trailer, cabin, shack, apartment, Victorian home, modern mansion, or castle. It is wise to first acknowledge and celebrate your relationship with the infinite. Pray, sing, and dance for the divine no matter your circumstances. Again, if you do these things in order to bring forth a desired outcome, you fail to live in the big room of mystery. If you only pray when you are in dire straits, then you are doing little more than dialing 911. If you pray because you desire to receive wealth and success, then you are only calling a financial consultant. Only when you pray to be right with God, surrendering your partialness to a greater whole wisdom, does prayer become transformative. Never forget that when holy bread is actually served, don't pause to ask whether it is gluten free.

The Flowing Light of God

On February 1, 2015, I dreamed that I was full of light and that it poured out of my mouth. I woke up hearing the words of the apostle Paul, "Once you were darkness, but now you are light in the Lord; walk as children of light" (Ephesians 5:8). You are called into the divine light where you are made a vessel through which this luminosity shines. This spiritual classroom led me to learning about the mystic, Mechthild of Magdeburg. In her collection of prose and verse, *The Flowing Light of the Godhead*, she writes, "The Godhead is so firey hot. Heaven's glow and all the holy lights flow from His divine breath and human mouth by the counsel of the Holy Spirit."[50] She, too, saw her visionary teaching as a mystical light coming through her mouth.

Mechthild regarded the personal experience of God as involving a mutual interaction between the heart of God and the human heart. For her, the *unio mystica*, the moment in which your lovesick soul receives fulfillment through uniting with the beloved divine, is a two-way affair. God longs for the human soul as much as the latter longs for divinity. During Mechthild's lifetime in the 1200s, this was a new and radical idea for Christianity. She taught that God will come close to you to the extent that you allow your heart to open. In this sacred courtship between the human and divine, God woos its longed-for soul:

> When God sees fit to let his divine heart shine forth in love toward the blessed soul so intensely that a small spark alights on the cold soul and she receives so much that the heart of this person begins to glow, his soul to melt, and his eyes to flow, then our Lord would like to make an earthly person so heavenly that one actually wants to follow, love, and see God in him.[51]

Later she writes:

> Whoever wishes to speak more about this,
> Let him prostrate himself in this fire
> And see and taste how the Godhead flows,
> How humanity pours,
> How the Holy Spirit wrestles,
> And vanquishes many a heart,
> Forcing it to love God intensely.[52]

After many encounters of blissful union and rapture with God, you are left with the ultimate gift: the never-ending longing for God, the "blessed longing." Anyone "entangled in longing such as this must forever hang blessedly fettered in God."[53] As a

Bushman doctor would say, you are now "owned by God" and "you own God," meaning that you are emotionally tied together forever more. This "marriage" is the bringing together of masculine and feminine, Sky God and trickster, heaven and earth, the sacred and profane, as well as all other holy couplings. You and the divine are married in the light and song of the mystical bridal chamber. The Gnostics found this room to be holier than a baptismal pool, because here is found union with the Godhead.

The bridal mysticism of Saint Mechthild created a new kind of poetry that evokes the mystic's passionate, ecstatic experience of God. Her writing inspired so much criticism during her time that some authorities called for it to be burned. However, the fire in Mechthild's heart burned with more heat than any earthly fire and its flames were never extinguished; her passion for God remains alive today inside her words:

1
Lord, you are my lover,
My longing,
My flowing stream,
My sun,
And I am your reflection.

2
The day
of my spiritual awakening
was the day I saw —
and knew I saw —
all things in God
and God in all things.

3
Love your fellow beings —
for they are all
tabernacles of God.

4

Of all that God has shown me,
I can speak just the smallest word,
not more than a honeybee takes on her foot
from an overspilling jar.

5

In the fire of creation,
gold does not vanish,
the fire brightens.
Each creature God made
must live in its own true nature,
how could I resist my nature,
that lives for oneness with God?

6

The Holy Spirit is our Harpist;
all strings which are touched in Love, must sound.

7

I cannot dance, Lord,
unless you lead me.
If you want me to leap with abandon,
You must intone the song.
Then I shall leap into love,
From love into knowledge,
From knowledge into enjoyment,
And from enjoyment
beyond all human sensations.
There I want to remain,
yet want also to circle higher still.

8

I who am Divine am truly in you.
I can never be sundered from you:
However far we be parted,

never can we be separated.
I am in you and you are in Me.
We could not be any closer.
We two are fused into one,
poured into a single mould.
Thus, unwearied,
we shall remain forever.

9

I, God, am your playmate!
I will lead the child in you in wonderful ways
for I have chosen you.
Beloved child, come swiftly to Me
for I am truly in you.
Then I shall leap into love.

10

How should one live?
Live welcoming to all.

11

When are we like God? I will tell you.
In so far as we love compassion and practice it
steadfastly,
to that extent do we resemble the heavenly Creator
who practices these things ceaselessly in us.

12

I who am Divine am truly in you.
I can never be sundered from you:
However far we be parted, never can we be
separated.
I am in you and you are in Me.
We could not be any closer.
We two are fused into one,
poured into a single mould.
Thus, unwearied, we shall remain forever.

13

O you pouring God in your gift!
O you flowing God in your love!
O you burning God in your desire!
O you melting God in the union with your beloved!
O you resting God on my breasts!
Without you I cannot exist.

14

Do not fear your death.
For when that moment arrives,
I will draw my breath
and your soul will come to Me
like a needle to a magnet.[54]

The Universe Is a Song

Soon after the vision of light, I went to a spiritual classroom and heard a voice proclaim, "The universe is a song." The mystical teacher who said this was not seen, only heard. When others in the room tried to expound on this teaching with thoughtful comments like, "the Hindu universe sings Om," or "the universe has structure, qualities, and resemblances to that of a song," the voice repeated over and over, "The universe is a song."

I woke up wondering how the universe is a song, and eventually fell asleep only to dream the same dream again. The invisible teacher continued saying, "The universe is a song."

In this classroom I learned that your life is a song that improvises and embellishes its various melodic lines. You are not merely a story, nor can you be reduced to habits of construing meaning or being a representative of preferred ideologies and interpretations. You do not solely reside inside a word universe, though trickster may lure you to believe this is so. The universe — and therefore you and all of life inside it — is a song. Once you experience this deeply, you will find the source of spirit, joy, and love. [j]

Your simultaneous longing for God's love and God's longing to share divine love brings you closer to the heavenly music that is inseparable from the holiest light. Bernard of Clairvaux

---

[j] Here is found the source of impoverishment and failure for practically all schools of therapy and life coaching. No matter how much practitioners may claim to differ, they all reside inside the same house of spoken knowing, what the Kalahari Bushmen call "Second Creation." Here the emphasis is upon talk — talking about talk (conversation-focused approaches), talking about action (behavior-focused approaches), talking about thinking (cognitive-focused approaches) or talking about interpretation that maintains a story line (narrative-focused approaches), or some eclectic mash-up of all of these orientations. The impoverishment induced by making talk primary cannot be cured by any talking cure. In other words, the heart cannot be warmed and awakened when the medium of change remains in the chilled expression of trickster words.

When ecstatically ignited, the heart opens its door to the transformative power of creation that is unfettered by the limited understanding offered by categorical encapsulation. Past all talk is the realm of experience that the Bushmen call "First Creation." The latter is signaled by the spontaneous emergence of heartfelt song. Without song, there can be no healing that deeply matters. Ecstatic healing points to what lies beyond therapy and life coaching. In the most spiritually heated ways of healing, there is no need for talk. In the less heated forms, talk is alive and present as metaphor and creative poetics. Without any spiritual warmth, there is only the chilled and shrunken context of Second Creation.

The tundra of frozen, static words, categorical knowing, and totalizing interpretations constructs and maintains the ground of suffering. The more a therapist or life coach exalts the words that construe and make true the importance of narrative, reflection, and interpretation, the more the pathological context of suffering is held in place. A session comes alive only when practitioners turn up the spiritual temperature and initiate movement toward the vast room of First Creation. We therefore call for the end of psychotherapy and coaching as they have been practiced in Second Creation. Let's move the helping professions out of the deadbeat, reified principles of a pseudo-social science and imitative allopathic medicine, and re-situate them in the performing arts held inside the creative fire of vast sacred mystery.

describes this special mystical song of illumined union:

> But there is that other song, which, by its unique
> dignity and sweetness, excels all those I have
> mentioned and any others there might be; hence by
> every right do I acclaim it as the *Song of Songs*. It
> stands at a point where all the others culminate. Only
> the touch of the Spirit can inspire a song like this, and
> only personal experience can unfold its meaning. Let
> those who are versed in the mystery revel in it; let all
> others burn with desire rather to attain to this
> experience than merely to learn about it. For it is a
> melody that resound abroad by the very music of the
> heart, not a trilling on the lips but an inward pulsing
> of delight, a harmony not of voices but of wills. It is a
> tune you will not hear in the streets, these notes do
> not sound where crowds assemble; only the singer
> hears it and the one to whom he sings — the lover and
> the beloved. It is preeminently a marriage song telling
> of chaste souls in loving embrace, of their wills in
> sweet accord, of the mutual exchange of the heart's
> affection.[55]

S. O. Fawzi, in his dissertation titled *Mystical Interpretation of
the Song of Songs in the Light of Ancient Jewish Mysticism*, proposes:

> The most important literary product of Merkabah
> mysticism is the Hekhalot literature which describes
> the ascent to the divine chariot. The texts of the
> Hekhalot refer to the celestial palaces through which
> the mystic passes until he reaches the seventh palace
> where he encounters the divine figure and the glory
> of His throne. Also alongside the descriptive material
> are hymns or incantations recited by the ascenders or
> heard by them through their heavenly journey. The

recitation of these hymns helps the mystic to pass through the gates of the palaces which are usually guarded by angels. . . . The Hekhalot hymns occupy a prominent place in these texts, particularly in Hekhalot Rabbati where they display some extravagant enthusiasm and a rhythmical approach in the praises of God, his power, greatness and benevolence. These hymns seem to be a collection possibly derived from some unknown or lost schools of mystics.[56]

The mysterious Song of Songs gives poetic expression to the highest yearning for love, and is cherished by mystics who experience intimate closeness to divinity. The celestial music heard by ecstatically awakened mystics and shamans, as well as the great musical composers, points toward intensely felt sounds and rhythms. It is the call and response of the highest emotion, communion, union, and love. What difference does it make to move from word to sound, story to song, and narrative to music? This movement constitutes the walk toward mystery—doing so step by step, note by note, and song by song. This is climbing the rope to God, a journey of vibratory sound whose sanctified music awakens heartfelt spiritual awareness. Only song enables the emotions of the heart to rise above the chatter of mind.

Receiving a Mysterious Password to Joseph Hart

On February 2, 2015, I had a most unusual visionary dream in which I saw a piece of paper with a single word on it that I did not recognize: *sojoprings*. I immediately woke up and wrote it down. I entered the word into a Google search; it produced only one result.[57] It was actually a mistyping of the word "sufferings," as found in an old hymn written for the Holy Communion or The Lord's Supper. The hymn, composed by Joseph Hart, is titled "The Blest Memorials of Thy Grief." It appeared in hymnbooks from about 1790 until 1890.[58] Here are the original lyrics (italicized words are ours):

> The blest memorials of thy grief,
> The suff'rings [spelled "sojoprings"] of thy death,
> We come, dear Savior, to receive,
> But would receive with *faith*.
>
> The tokens sent us to relieve
> Our spirits, when they droop,
> We come, dear Savior, to receive,
> But would receive with *hope*.
>
> The pledges, thou wast pleas'd to leave
> Our mournful minds to move,
> We come, dear Savior, to receive,
> But would receive with *love*.
>
> Here, in obedience to thy word,
> We take the bread and wine;
> The utmost we can do, dear Lord,
> For *all beyond* is thine.[59]

In this hymn, Hart tracks the progressive movement of faith, hope, love, and the communion that is *all beyond* human comprehension. First turn to the memorials of the holy death and resurrection that include scripture, prayer, painted icon, and carved crucifix. As you are reminded of how suffering and death were spiritually conquered, you find *faith*. Second, when you experience your spirit drooping and waning, unexpected symbolic tokens of divine presence help bring *hope*. Third, while mourning the suffering of the divine beloved, you are touched by God's unbroken pledge to deliver *love* to all who are broken. Finally, with faith, hope, and love, you are inspired to obediently take your stand upon the hallowed words of sacred ground ("thy word") where Holy Communion is received. Here whatever takes place, and this includes admission to the higher mysteries, is determined by God. With each of these gifts, you advance your relationship with the divine, climbing the rope to God. *Beyond* faith is hope, and then love, all steps leading toward the ultimate mystery.

Before this dream, I had never heard of Joseph Hart (1712–1768); most people today have not heard of him, either. I discovered that he was a Calvinist minister in London whose hymnbook, *Hart's Hymns*, was popular for many years among evangelicals. He was heralded as "the most spiritual of the English hymn-writers" and over 20,000 people attended his funeral at Bunhill Fields in London. Yet in spite of this impact, hardly anyone in our time knows this man's name or work. Brian Golez Najapfour notes: "In fact, since 1910, no major biography has been written about him, and, since 1988, no major article on him has been published. His hymns, even among evangelical churches, are rarely sung."[60]

As I researched Joseph Hart, I discovered that the only remaining book he wrote is now out of print; it is titled *Hymns Composed on Various Subjects.*[61] It contains a brief autobiographical preface that is arguably one of the most outstanding spiritual testimonies ever written. Called "A Brief and Summary Account of the Author's Experience and the Great Things that God Hath Done for His Soul," Hart presents the stages of spiritual growth he went through—matching what is presented in the above hymn—and doing so truthfully, with heart-touching emotion and exquisite clarity.[62]

Hart was a scholar of classics and translator of religious texts, and his intellectual integrity and literary background gave him a superb critical mind. He yearned, however, to transcend intellectual understanding of scripture and more deeply penetrate the mystery behind Christianity. Hart found that he needed to go past belief and good works and be transformed by a mystical encounter with God. Hart's first revelation, inspired by being transfixed on the agony of Christ in the garden, took place later in his life. He describes it as follows in his autobiography:

> The week before Easter, 1757, I had such an amazing view of the agony of Christ in the garden, as I know not well how to describe. I was lost in wonder and adoration, and the impression it made was too deep, I believe, ever to be obliterated. I shall say no more of this, but only remark that notwithstanding all that is talked about the sufferings of Jesus, none can know anything of them but by the Holy Ghost; and I believe he that knows most knows very little. It was upon this I made the first part of hymn 1, *On the Passion*.[63]

Though this revelation brought him closer to divine mystery, it also precipitated his fear about how God's overwhelming immensity could reconcile with his personal shortcomings and the broken pledges he had made to God, something constantly reminded to him by scripture. Hart's continuous struggle with his own character became another roadblock in his spiritual development. He listened to many sermons, seeking further direction and solace, yet continued to desperately long for something beyond words: "*Notions of religion* I wanted no man to teach me: I had *doctrine* enough, but found by woeful experience, that *dry doctrine*, though ever so sound will not sustain a soul in the day of trial."[64] Hart's post-visionary anguish eventually led to what he called his true conversion, a "re-conversion," which he describes as follows:

> I was hardly got home [from attending a sermon at Moravian Chapel] when I felt myself melting away into a strange softness of affection, which made me fling myself on my knees before God. My horrors were immediately dispelled, and such light and

comfort flowed into my heart, as no words can paint. The Lord by His Spirit of love came, not in a visionary manner into my *brain* but with such divine power and energy into my *soul* that I was lost in blissful amazement. I cried out, "What *ME*, Lord?" His Spirit answered in me, "Yes, YOU!" I objected, "But I have been so unspeakably vile and wicked!" The answer was, "I pardon you fully and freely. Your own *goodness* (for I had now set about a thorough amendment, if perhaps I might be spared) cannot save you, nor shall your *wickedness* damn you. I undertake to work all your words in you and for you; and to bring you safely through all."

The alteration I then felt in my soul was as sudden and palpable as that which is experienced by a person staggering, and almost sinking, under a burden, when it is immediately taken from his shoulders. Tears ran in streams from my eyes for a considerable while; and I was so swallowed up in joy and thankfulness, that I hardly knew where I was. I threw my soul willingly into my Savior's hands; lay weeping at His feet, wholly resigned to His will, and only begging that I might, if He was graciously pleased to permit it be of some service to His Church and people.

Thenceforth I enjoyed sweet peace in my soul; and had such clear and frequent manifestations of His love to me, that I longed for no other heaven. My horrors were banished, and have not, I think, returned since with equal violence.[65]

To grasp the power of Hart's mystical conversion experience one must look to the wider context of his spiritual path. Like many people who set out to walk the straight and narrow road,

Hart found himself oscillating between two unfulfilling choices. Namely, he found that belief alone was not sufficient, because a profession of faith could easily be used as an excuse for living an undisciplined life. On the other hand, Hart realized that emphasizing "good works" and moral conduct also fell short of fostering a more profound communion with God. He writes of his spiritual state prior to his vision:

> For several years I went on in this easy, cool, smooth, and indolent manner with a lukewarm, insipid kind of religion; yet not without some secret whispers of God's love, and visitations of His grace, and now and then warm addresses to Him in private prayer. But, alas, all this while, my heart was unbroken.[66]

Regardless of your spiritual orientation, there is always the question of whether you are "walking the talk" — and whether too much emphasis on the latter renders you an overly judgmental gatekeeper of moral codes. But Hart points to the bigger concern of whether you have been radically transformed through a direct experience of divine ecstasy, something that requires existentially hitting bottom with a broken heart. Hart's testimony clearly articulates how we may avoid the latter condition by staying afloat in "this easy, cool, smooth, and indolent manner with a lukewarm, insipid kind of religion." As Hart found, however, if you want to be deeply touched by divine grace and find your way to the only source that can truly quench your spiritual hunger and thirst, you must allow your heart, as well as the safety walls built by trickster mind, to be broken.

As my earlier vision taught, the question that must be asked is, "Are you broken yet?" Hillary and I accordingly advise our students that they must go past the false comfort of "lukewarm" spiritual practice and presumptuous know-it-all-ism in order to break down all walls of resistance and make enough room for

God. As Hart found, this is when you are penetrated by the "divine power and energy" that brings "blissful amazement" and "sweet peace" to the soul, the pinnacle experience of being spiritually cooked that ecstatics have sought and found throughout history.

What stands out in Hart's reconversion testimony are the words he heard from God, speaking to the core of what had been his spiritual struggle: "Your own *goodness* . . . cannot save you, nor shall your *wickedness* damn you. I undertake to work all your words in you and for you; and to bring you safely through all." This counsel renders the comparative measurement of goodness and wickedness irrelevant. Faced with the realization that being good cannot help and wickedness cannot hurt, the mind must surrender itself to some greater spiritual force that is not reachable through any simple either/or. Hart later articulated this teaching as follows, in what became his personal motto:

> *Pharisaic zeal* and *Antinomian security*[k] are the two engines of Satan, with which he grinds the church in all ages, as betwixt [between] the upper and the nether [lower] millstone. The space between them is much narrower and harder to find than most men imagine. It is a path which the vulture's eye hath not seen; and none can show it us but the Holy Ghost.[67]

Though cast in Christian metaphor, Hart points to the basic spiritual tension underlying all lineages of ecstatic spirituality. Neither correct thought and belief nor exemplary action is

---

[k] Pharisaic zeal (referring to the Pharisees) is an enthusiasm for following and enforcing religious law. In contrast, "antinomian" refers to Christians who believe that the grace of God bestowed upon the faithful exempts them from the obligations of adhering to religious law in order to receive salvation. Put simply, pharisaic zeal and antinomian security represent for Joseph Hart two extremes: on one side an overemphasis on adhering to religious precepts and on the other an overemphasis on faith alone at the expense of disciplined action.

enough to bring a spiritual breakthrough. Rather than be content with doctrine in your head or perfectly performed piety, there is a need for the spirit to be revealed to your heart. Being nearer the divine requires escaping the forced choice to elevate either thought or deed. What is inescapably needed is complete surrender to the Creator, the Lord of all creation. At that moment, you are whisked away and thrown into the ecstatic fire. While we have been taught to avoid the devil's fire of hell, we have also been, perhaps accidentally, taught to avoid the heavenly fire of God. The path to divine ecstasy is found in the narrow space between all contradictions conceived by mind, a trail that is in Hart's words "too fine for man to discern."[68] Mind cannot see what it cannot distinguish; therefore, you need God to show you the way.

Whenever "correct thinking" is emphasized you will fall short of the mystical glory. Similarly, all the spiritual achievements in the world—from sweat lodge attendance to sun dancing, whirling dervish participation, long fasts, prayer meetings, baptisms, and the endurance of countless ordeals and initiations—won't necessarily help. Spiritual knowledge and accomplishment may actually impede your advancement if you haven't come to the gate with a broken heart that is ready to be handed over to God. Are you broken yet? If not, then look again. Behind all your talk and walk, there is a heart waiting to be made whole by the divine. Without brokenness, you can't advance one inch on the spiritual highway.

Joseph Hart became a preacher at Jewin Street meeting-place or chapel in London and his hymns and sermons inspired Charles Spurgeon, whose own hymnbook included 17 hymns by Hart. Peter C. Rae writes:

> It is true of the hymns of Hart, and the theology contained within them, that he believed that the heart of Christian experience was not merely the

acceptance of certain doctrines or a system of dogmatics, but a living and vital relationship with the Lord.[69]

Not surprisingly, Hart only started writing hymns after his first personal mystical experience. While most of his other writing disappeared and is presumed lost, the hymns that survived celebrate the universal love of Jesus. Again, he emphasized that such bliss is only possible through contact with the holy spirit:

> The Holy Ghost will make the soul
> Feel its sad condition:
> For the sick and not the whole,
> Need the good Physician.[70]

In his most famous hymn, Hart describes the reconversion that involves a true change of heart and reception of God's grace:

> Come, ye sinners, poor and wretched,
> Weak and wounded, sick and sore, . . .
>
> Let not conscience make you linger,
> Nor of fitness fondly dream;
> All the fitness He requireth
> Is to feel your need of Him:
> This He gives you, this He gives you, this He
>   gives you;
> 'Tis the Spirit's rising beam.
>
> Come, ye weary, heavy laden,
> Bruis'd and mangled by the fall;
> If you tarry till you're better,
> You will never come at all!
> Not the righteous, not the righteous, not the
>   righteous;
> Sinners, Jesus came to call. . . .

Saints and angels, join'd in concert,
Sing the praises of the Lamb;
While the blissful seats of Heaven
Sweetly echo with His name;
Hallelujah! Hallelujah! Hallelujah!
Sinners here may sing the same.[71]

Hart reminds us that what is most important is to *feel your need for divinity*, rather than pronounce belief or posture goodness. Being weak, wounded, sick, poor, weary, heavy laden, bruised, or mangled, rather than displaying righteousness or "fitness," paradoxically empowers the voyage to ecstasy. Hart's life serves as testimony that unless you deeply feel a desperate need for divine intervention, you are not ready to hear the concert of the saints and angels. The ultimate divine paradox is that you must be small in order to be admitted to it All, *and* you must offer up your suffering in order for the alchemy of God to convert it into ecstatic joy.

In addition, Hart radically invites you to go further than your own suffering and suggests that you also face the suffering that took place in "sad Gethsemane." He writes: "Come all ye chosen saints of God, That long to feel the cleansing blood; In pensive pleasure join with me, To sing of sad Gethsemane."[72] To go deeper into divine mystery, Hart prescribes prayer to "feel the effects of Jesus' death."[73] In other words, pray to intimately experience the mysterious transformation of suffering into the highest joy, of death into renewed life, and of a broken human part and heart into the sacred whole. Hart writes:

> Not long after this my — shall I call it *re-conversion*? . . .
> I feel myself now as poor, as weak, as helpless and dependent as ever; but now my *weakness* is my *greatest strength*; I now rejoice, though I rejoice with trembling.[74]

Your spiritual correctness will not help you, nor will your unruly misconduct damn you. No matter what you have done or not done, when you face divinity you are pardoned and set free from any existential jail. Only when you stand in the big room of mystery and receive your pardon do mystical gifts arrive through the revolving door of opposites. Whatever was true in the small spaces of trickster mind becomes reversed in infinite sacred space. Your weakness becomes your greatest strength, evil is swallowed by good, death re-enters life, and every part becomes inseparable from the whole. All of this is felt as you "drink deeper and deeper" of the "cup of salvation" that contains all spiritual treasure.[75]

Amongst the Littleness: Choosing the Low, Despised Mystery

By his young adulthood, Joseph Hart had mastered the languages of French, Hebrew, Greek, and Latin. His scholarship in the literature of ancient Rome and Greece resulted in the translation of the poem "Phycolides" in 1744 and Herodian's history of Rome in 1749, now held in the University Library at Cambridge and the British Museum, respectively. During this time he could be found in the day "bending over the dingy bookstalls of the Moorfields," where as a classics scholar he went past trivial analysis and found he could absorb and express the essence of the author's outlook. Hart's biographer, Thomas Wright, noted his secret to unraveling the ancient mysteries: "He laid down that as with other temples, so with the classics, it is love alone that unlocks." However, his pursuit of spiritual knowledge left him unsatisfied as he thought of himself as an "insensate mariner" who "sees yet strikes the shelf."[76]

As he turned to study the Bible in all its translations, he also attempted "the quixotic task of endeavoring to form a homogeneous whole out of incompatible materials." He believed that "the external evidence of all religions is much the same. But the internal evidence of pure Christianity is invincible. I mean the divine doctrines of salvation and universal charity." Though he concluded that "the Bible well deserves the title of the best book extant" and was a "repository of sweet treasures,"[77] he relentlessly tried to find commonalities with other religious teachings. One example of the parallels he found in diverse religions is Hart's examination of the ecstatic ceremonies that honor the Mother Goddess, Cybele:

> However odd and fantastic these dancing festivals among the heathen may seem to us moderns, I cannot but observe that there is in them a strong resemblance of some in use among the Jews. . . . King David is described dancing before the ark in a very extraordinary manner. . . . Even the frantic behaviour of the priests of this goddess, in their mad processions at her festivals . . . is equalled by the phrenzy of the Jewish prophets.[78]

Hart also studied the magicians of pagan times, the Magi, and concluded that they had accessed power and visionary knowledge: "That miracles may be performed by magicians and prophets of heterodox principles is plain from the story of the Egyptian conjurers, who, as well as Moses, produced several plagues."[79]

What characterized Hart's translations was his faithfulness to honest and clear representation of the author's words. As his biographer noted, "it pleased him more to make tremendous dissertations on grammatical niceties."[80] Yet when he strove to unlock the truths of the Bible, he grew frustrated with his own limitations in deciphering. As his biographer said,

> His notes are cumbrous with quotations from the Hebrew, to say nothing of the Greek, but, with all his erudition, the Bible was as yet a sealed book to him. He had still something to learn which mountains of

Hebrew and oceans of Greek were incapable of imparting.[81]

What was sealed from Hart? What was missing in his experience as he intellectually explored different religions? He found magic and miracles in all of them, as well as ecstatic experience. However, he specifically noted that what made the doctrines of the Bible unique involved its means of salvation and universal charity. *Salvation*, in a most general sense, means deliverance from a vicious life cycle where no matter what someone thinks or does, he or she feels that something vital is missing. Hart's autobiographical testimony reveals that salvation to him is release from the bondage and prison of mind, both the arrogant certainty and the doubting chatter that leave you "lukewarm" and absent of sacred emotion. Hart experienced agony as he became more aware of how he was lost, drifting further away from the promises and pledges he had personally made to Jesus: "I broke His law, and (worse than that) Alas! I broke His heart."[82] When he heard the great evangelist George Whitefield preach at a public gathering, he observed people falling into great emotion, cries, and bodily movement, calling it a "wild fire." Witnessing this ecstatic expression brought on further despondency because Hart was fully aware that he "had never experienced grand revelations and miraculous discoveries." As he said:

> I was very melancholy and shunned all company, walking pensively alone or sitting in private and bewailing my sad and dark condition, not having a friend in the world to whom I could communicate the burden of my soul, which was so heavy that I sometimes hesitated even to take my necessary food.[83]

Hart recognized then that all his intellectual attempts to

understand magic, literature, comparative religions, and the Bible fell short of having a direct mystical experience, something confirmed by the emotional bliss it awakens. Only such a pinnacle spiritual experience could free him from the encapsulation of a life centered on mind alone. As Hart describes, he spent many hours in sorrowful prayer with "frequent cries and tears to God . . . beseeching Him to reveal Himself to me in a clearer manner." In the midst of one of these episodes, Hart recounts that he heard the voice of God ask, "whether I rather chose the visionary revelations of which I had formed some wild idea, or to be content with trusting to the low, despised mystery of a crucified man?" Hart began, according to his recollection, "pouring out my soul to Christ, and beseeching Him, with cries and groans and tears, to reveal Himself to me."[84]

Then came the most important event of his life—Hart had his first mystical vision where he experienced Jesus in the garden of Gethsemane. We repeat his report of this vision so it can be read again, knowing the context of his life at the time it took place:

> The week before Easter, 1757, I had such an amazing view of the agony of Christ in the garden as I know not well how to describe. I was lost in wonder and adoration, and the impression it made was too deep, I believe, ever to be obliterated. I shall say no more of this, but only remark that, notwithstanding all that is talked about the sufferings of Jesus, none can know anything of them but by the Holy Ghost; and I believe he that knows most knows but very little.[85]

While we know that the vision led him to write his first hymn, "On the Passion," it is less known that Hart later mentioned that he actually revised what he originally wrote, saying that the version we know today is "mutilated" by his alteration.[86] It is likely that he assumed that the spiritual power of his original verse was too much for others to bear. His vision and hymn aimed to "enter into the deep mysteries of Gethsemane, and the intense reality of the sufferings."[87] In this hymn he represents the "Lord as bearing all that incarnate God could bear, 'With strength enough, and none to spare.'" As his biographer concluded, "none but a soul fluctuating between mortal agony and divine rapture could possibly have penned it."[88] Like Beethoven, Hart was suspended between heaven and hell, and in this gap was found ecstasy. Like Jesus, he had taken all the suffering he could handle and was at the breaking point. At that instant Hart was penetrated by "the low, despised mystery," wherein the greatest moment of weakness is found the most intense and profound experience of the strength of God's love.

After Hart's vision of Gethsemane and his reconversion experience he wrote:

> I soon began to be visited by God's Spirit in a different manner from what I had ever felt before. I had constant *communion* with Him in prayer. His sufferings, His wounds, His agonies of soul were impressed upon me in an amazing manner. I now believed my name was sculptured deep in the Lord Jesus' breast, with engraving never to be erased. I saw Him with the eye of faith, stooping under the load of my sins; groaning and groveling in Gethsemane for me. The incarnate God was more and more revealed to me; and I had far other notions of His sufferings than I had entertained before. . . .
>
> I had also such a spirit of sympathetic love to the Lord Jesus given me—that after I had left off to sorrow for *myself*, for some months I grieved and mourned bitterly for *Him*. I looked on Him whom I had pierced, and felt such sharp compunction, mixed at the same time with so much compassion, that the

pain and the pleasure I experienced, are much better *felt* – than *expressed.*

Jesus Christ, and Him crucified, is now the only thing I desire to know. In that *incarnate mystery* is contained all the rich treasures of divine wisdom. This is the mark toward which I am still pressing forward. This is the cup of salvation, of which I wish to drink deeper and deeper. This is the knowledge in which I long to grow; and desire at the same time a daily increase in all true grace and godliness. All duties, works, ordinances, etc. are to me then only rich—when they are enriched with the blood of the Lamb, in comparison of which all things else are but chaff and husks![89]

Hart uncovered the same kind of relationship to mystery as that of other cooked mystics and spiritual ecstatics. Namely, a constant communion with divinity that is deeply felt rather than just intellectually understood. It's essential to again underscore that it was Joseph Hart's choice to trust "the low, despised mystery" of Jesus on the cross that allowed him to break through the "chaff and husks" of intellect and receive the deepest communion with God.

While the names and metaphors may differ over time and across religious traditions, the underlying principles and patterns of interaction between human beings and divinity remain the same. Today, the New Age spiritual marketplace tempts you to chase "the visionary revelations of which you have formed a wild idea," to use Hart's phrase. Such grasping feeds the discontent of self-aggrandizement, insulating you against the incompleteness and brokenness that are needed to experience the peace and joy of your littleness in the midst of the infinite.

When one experiences the heavenly expansion that comes with the recognition of smallness, the transformation is so profound that even "the blood of the Lamb," as Hart suggests, transforms from a symbol of horror to something that enriches and gives life to our spiritual walk.

Hart discovered that the full teaching of Jesus's life cannot be penetrated without coming face to face with the mystery of the crucifixion. In a mourning ceremony among the Spiritual Baptists (Shakers) of St. Vincent, I was sent in vision to Calvary where I witnessed Jesus nailed and hung on the cross. A voice whispered, "Jump!" and when I jumped, I was immediately thrown into the body of the crucified one. Like Hart, I felt Jesus's deep sadness about the human condition and how this brought more suffering than the physical pain inflicted on his body. I was shown how this horrific ordeal was required to break his heart so that he, too, could cross the bridge between flesh and spirit. In his case, the bridge was made for all human beings to find a way to cross over to the higher realm, enabling their humanity to be touched by divinity.

Like Reverend Joseph Hart and other mystical journeyers in St. Vincent (and throughout the world), I found that the low, despised mystery was the highest mystery of them all. During the historical time of Jesus, there was no more shameful punishment than crucifixion; the Roman authorities did not want to inflict it on him because he had not committed the kind of crime that warranted it. This fatal torture was demanded by the public and its religious authorities, who were upset that Jesus had failed to overthrow a political regime. Instead, he came to overthrow "pharisaic zeal and antinomian security" to show how love and brokenheartedness open the door to the kingdom, power, and glory of God.

Hart concludes his brief autobiography by elaborating how he partakes in the ongoing transformation of communion that longs for union:

Though poor in myself—I am rich enough in Him.

When my dry, empty, barren soul is parched with
thirst, He kindly bids me come to Him, and drink my
fill at the fountainhead. In a word, He empowers me
to say, with experimental evidence, "Where sin
abounded, grace doth much more abound." Amen
and amen![90]

Hart constantly reminds us that only an intensely felt
relationship with the holy spirit, a rope to God, can reveal the
truth of ineffable mystery. Hart's vision opened "the mysteries of
His cross," declaring it the highest compass setting for his
mystical life: "Jesus Christ, and Him crucified, is now the only
thing I desire to know."[91] There at the crossing of life and death
is found the flowing water, blood, and spirit of eternal life. In his
hymn for communion, the one whose misspelled word brought
us to this forgotten psalmist of God, Hart celebrated the ultimate
spiritual journey from faith to hope, to love, and finally to that
which is "all beyond" because it "is thine." The latter
communion with the holy spirit is where Hart found fulfillment:
"Though poor in myself—I am rich enough in Him. When my
dry, empty, barren soul is parched with thirst—He kindly bids
me come to Him, and drink my fill at the fountain head."

The more Joseph Hart fasted and followed spiritual rules and
laws, the more he was aware of his distance from the ecstatic
mystery of Jesus. The more Hart studied the Bible and other
religions with a disciplined scholarship known to few, the more
he fell upon his knees, as it became clearer he did not embody
that to which he had pledged his faith and committed himself to
study. On the lowest ground, he finally surrendered and was
given a vision and rope to God that brought holy song and
ecstatic entry into what is otherwise an unattainable mystery.

During this time of studying Joseph Hart, I had another
dream:

Hillary and I were at one of our favorite old hotels

attending a family reunion. I took a walk with my father to tell him that visions were pouring through us every night and had not stopped. I then started to tell him about Joseph Hart. As I began recounting Hart's first vision about Gethsemane, I was so overcome with emotion that I convulsed with tears. I woke up from the dream remembering what my father had taught me when I was a child.

While attending church at around twelve years of age, my father explained that Gethsemane was a place located on a slope of Mount Olive, across the Kidron Valley of Jerusalem. On the night before the crucifixion, Jesus brought the disciples there, a place where they often gathered to pray together. Each of the Gospel writers made an account of what transpired. That evening Jesus took aside his three main disciples, Peter, James, and John, and asked them to help him. "My soul is deeply grieved, to the point of death; remain here and keep watch with me" (Matthew 26:38). He then walked a bit further from them and fell to his face. In agony, Jesus asked God to find another way. His sweat fell like drops of blood and though he found it difficult to accept God's will, he surrendered to it. An angel was sent to comfort him. While Jesus wept in anguish, Peter, James, and John fell asleep. "So, you men could not keep watch with me for one hour? Keep watching and praying, that you may not enter into temptation; the spirit is willing, but the flesh is weak" (Matthew 26:40–41). They soon fell asleep again.

In my dream, my father and I were brought to tears when we imagined the kind of heartbreak Jesus must have felt when his best disciples could not stay awake while he prayed. Imagine dedicating yourself to a great spiritual master teacher — and on your last night with him you are asked to stay awake as he prays before being unjustly sentenced to a brutal death. You are likely having your last intimate moment with someone who is undoubtedly a true vessel of miracles. You haven't been asked to stay awake all night; only for a few hours at most, long enough for the master to pray. Here you learn how easy it is to get distracted, even at the most important spiritual moment. Perhaps the disciples assumed that the heavenly father would take care of Jesus and send a supernatural rescue party, or that Jesus would wave a magic olive branch and everything would be back to normal. Maybe they assumed that Jesus was beyond the need for help from his fellow man. They missed that Jesus was not only the Son of God; he was also a human being who was suffering and needed help to get him through the night. Not a single disciple was able to follow his simple request.

Be humbled, knowing how fickle, weak, and easily led astray the human mind is and that it is no easy accomplishment to stay alert long enough or follow instructions passionately enough for God to do the work on you that is needed. Be compassionate with yourself, for there will be many times when you don't stay spiritually awake. The human tendency to easily fall asleep and become indolent brought remorse to Joseph Hart and the apostles as well. When you forsake your vows and fall off the path, take notice of it and immediately spiritually reboot to get back on track with your mission. You are here to be a sunbeam in the shadows, to illumine the way for others who are lost. When you fall into darkness, choose to recharge your spiritual batteries and turn the light back on, rather than fall into despair. As Hart said, where human shortcomings and all other manner of error abound, "grace doth much more abound."[92]

The Name that Stirs Emotion of One Kind or Another

Seldom does a name elicit such an emotional reaction as the name of Jesus. It either inspires devotion, repulsion, or both—depending upon the social setting and spiritual temperature. Hillary and I, for example, feel less enthusiastic about hearing this name when uttered by cold judgmental Christians who are more dogmatically incensed than they are filled with divine love. However, in the heat of an old-school sanctified praise meeting, we delight in hearing and shouting his name. Unlike most holy names, the name of Jesus brings out incredibly strong, passionate emotion. Everyone can agree that this name is not easy to ignore. It is loaded with an energy that brings an intense response.

When people get upset upon hearing the name Jesus, we remind them that being too annoyed with a name indicates that they likely have an intimate relationship with it. Furthermore, as Carl Jung pointed out, you can suddenly become attracted to that which you oppose too much. In other words, too much protest leads to the love nest. It matters not whether you protest or nest. Either way, something has a hold on you.

Receiving the mysterious password to Joseph Hart brought us into relationship with the profound mystical teaching of the crucifixion. This brought Hillary out of her comfort zone because she had grown accustomed to turning away from any serious consideration of Jesus. After being moved by Joseph Hart's testimony, she wrote a letter to our students, describing her own changing relationship to Jesus over time:

> I grew up Catholic, but our family wasn't very religious. For a long time as a young adult I had a strong aversion to any talk of Jesus, and especially sin or repentance. At the same time, I was able to readily receive Buddhist teachings about "atonement" for wrongdoing, surrendering the ego, and awakening to the "interrelationship of all sentient beings." I was too organized by my own trickster mind's preferences and prejudices to see how this equated with Jesus' teachings of forgiveness and unconditional love. I conflated Christianity with all the horrific human behavior that has been and continues to be done in Jesus's name, even as I knew on an intellectual level

that such a conflation was simplistic and unfair. I was also a bit embarrassed by the overt expression of emotion and devotion expressed by some Christians. Buddhism, in contrast, is typically more reserved and absent of that kind of ecstatic, emotional display.

Zen Buddhism taught me that when you truly commit to any religious path, at some point you will have to wrestle with your ego and know-it-all-ism. Your preferences and presumptions will come to slap you in the face and you will have to reckon with them. One tricky way of avoiding this kind of shattering surrender is to stay on the tertiary edge of things, picking and choosing the parts of various traditions that you find pleasing and palatable while rejecting the rest. Specifically in our time this approach has resulted in a lot of pop pseudo-Buddhism, pseudo-Hinduism, and pseudo-shamanism flooding the bookstores, magazines, and Internet blogs. While I value a world where people are free to hunt for spiritual wisdom that touches their heart, people too easily reject a whole religious tradition based on the ignorant actions of only some of its practitioners. Past personal history of negative experiences is then used to justify an inflated sense of spiritual discernment. Such a person ends up being as spiritually cold and hard as the people against whom he or she protests. Ignorance, meanness, and greed are pervasive among human beings, regardless of their religion, secular philosophy, or cultural background. Thankfully, so are wisdom, love, and generosity.

Because I am as hard-headed and skeptical as Joseph Hart was, my whole perspective and relationship to both Jesus and ecstatic expression only changed once I began my life with Brad and he started giving me nails[1] of *n/om*. I like to say that I arrived at the Christian praise house by way of the Kalahari, an ecstatic tradition powerful enough to empty me of my stubborn prejudice and ignorance. I found that my aversion to the name Jesus spontaneously fell away, and learned firsthand that once you have been spiritually cooked, there is room in your heart for all religions and this includes all their similarities and differences.

For me, Jesus is inseparable from my main rope to mystery. I'm not suggesting that this outcome will or should be the same for everyone who gets cooked. I do know, however, that if you truly get spiritually cooked in the old-school Kalahari way you will not be able to hold onto your staunch preferences, however justified you think they might be. If you really want to be cooked then you must be ready to hand everything over. You can't decide beforehand what parts you want to keep and what parts you want to surrender.

You don't have to equally embrace or practice all religions; that is nothing more than another trickster preference for shallow eclecticism. If you want to walk a spiritual path, however, you cannot skip the

---

[1] Receiving a "nail" of *n/om* is a Bushman term for describing transmission of the universal life force, a sacred vibration that is physically felt in the body. Unless experienced, there is no way to adequately describe its reception other than to note that it spontaneously precipitates ecstatic trembling and shaking, awakens the intense sacred emotion of divine love, breaks down all conceptual walls of disbelief about the existence of a greater force and higher source, and is instantly recognized as a transformation of one's whole being. The Bushman usually pass on *n/om* through vibratory touch by someone who is spiritually on fire and singing a song inspired by a close relationship with the God of creation.

part where you hit bottom, face your ignorance and arrogance, and surrender your life. That process will change you. Once you are cooked you will have a rope to God that will allow you to see, taste, smell, hear, and feel spiritual heat and soft-heartedness no matter what tradition hosts it. You will still get lost and self-inflated at times, but you will learn to trust the pulling of your rope and its built-in spiritual thermometer more than the preferences and presumed understanding of your mind.

The construction of vast sacred ground welcomes a felt relationship with divine love and all those who have embodied it. Setting your soul on fire and getting spiritually cooked are not about inflating an abstraction that entices your mind, but heightening a felt emotion for an immortal beloved that opens your heart. Expanding an abstraction may only constrict your heart and leave little room for the experience of love. This tragic outcome arrives as easily for pharisaic Christians as it does their dogmatic opponents. Both are inflators of abstraction rather than expansionists of love.

Beware the hard and cold mind of prejudice, including the prejudice for or against any holy name. Unless you surrender your heart fully to the utmost divine mystery that surpasses all names, you won't become tender enough to be pierced by its arrows. Unless you pray with enough emotional vigor, you won't find the song that provides a divine hookup. Without a heart big enough to feel the love of an incarnated one, including Jesus, you will miss a trustworthy companion who will assist your journey to the highest sacred room.

You are invited to head toward the ship that is ready to sail on the vast mystical sea. As you approach its boarding gate, hear a voice asking you the same questions heard by Hart: "Do you choose the visionary revelations of which you have formed some

115

wild idea" or are you "content with trusting to the low, despised mystery of a crucified Man?" All aboard the ship that is bound for the extreme love and mystery of infinite glory!

Thy Mystery Be Done

We never know what spiritual classroom we will be sent to in vision. At times our journeys take us to the great Muslim teachings of Ibn al-'Arabi and other Muslim prophets. That's when Hillary and I wonder whether we are heading to Mecca and need a prayer rug. At other times, we are in the Hebrew world of Moses and the great Jewish prophets, especially the inner secrets of the Kabbalah as concerns the throne and wheel of Ezekiel, the ascent through the many realms, and the Song of Songs. At other times we are surprised to mystically meet scientists from M.I.T. and the experimental aesthetician Charles Henry, along with the Beat poet, William Burroughs. Throughout all of our visionary travels, we pray that "Thy mystery be done."

We were totally surprised to find ourselves inside the spiritual classroom of the all-but-forgotten hymn writer and London preacher, Joseph Hart. That we were led to him by the dream of a word that is not found in any dictionary, "sojoprings"—the misspelling of the word "sufferings" in one of his hymns—is truly unexplainable. We likely would not have bothered to examine Hart's work that closely had we not received a visionary connection to him through that incomprehensible word. The impossible probability of the latter motivated us to pay attention. At the time of the Joseph Hart vision—and the months that preceded and followed it—we were filled with the holy spirit each day and night. The intensity of these heated and supercharged spiritual experiences cooked us so much that we felt we were going through a deep mystical conversion much like Hart's. We knew our lives would never be the same as we further surrendered to being servants of the divine.

We took a pledge to welcome whatever spiritual mystery arrives, no matter what form in which it is delivered. We recognize that some people have preferences for and against certain religious traditions; we all live in a sea of names, or Second Creation, where preference and its twin brother, prejudice, coexist. Inside God's expanding spiritual house we emphasize that there is no boundary between the mystical truths delivered from a synagogue and those birthed upon Kalahari sand, in a mosque, or in a manger in Bethlehem.

This "open to higher will" mystical and ecstatic spirituality frees us to feast at a table where any mystic from the past or present may show up and be welcome as long as they are met underneath the canopy of divine illumination. We are not suggesting a trivial form of religious pluralism or secular philosophical eclecticism. Instead, we seek to be inside a heavenly mansion large enough to allow the unadulterated mystical voice of any mystic, saint, shaman, or spiritual teacher to be heard without pulling it apart from the whole tradition from which it comes.

After receiving the preaching of Joseph Hart we pondered whether we'd be sent back to his London meeting place or be shown another mysterious password that might lead us to another forgotten teacher. To our surprise, we both woke up the next night around three o'clock in the morning and started shaking together like Bushmen sharing *n/om* as Kalahari-born music arrived and stayed with us until sunrise. As always, we trust that the greater mind of the divine knows best what needs to come through the sacred pipeline.

Sacred Ecstatics is an invitation to what we sometimes call "experimental ecstatic mysticism" or "cooking experiments with God." In other words, we experiment with setting fire to our soulful relationship with divinity. We have no need to apologize to anyone for our love of Jesus any more than we need to apologize to fundamentalist Christians for our love of anything or anyone through which God chooses to deliver a truth—be it from another wisdom lineage, rain drop, wind breeze, bee hive, sting, or honey. We love the mystics of Persia, Africa, the Amazon, the Arctic, the Caribbean, the Mississippi Delta, and the Holy Land, among other locales, as well as polishers of mind from Kyoto to London, Paris, and Cambridge. Furthermore, we welcome and embrace the sacred clowns, absurdists, *heyokas*, jesters, and holy fools, as we do all the instruments of the divine symphony.

Our *seiki* bench, Kalahari dance ground, life force theatre, shaking medicine clinic, and sanctified church pew are large enough to include any and all voices of the highest mystery. We invite you to step onto the stage of the greatest mystery show. Become a mystical sound and movement of the song-and-dance-universe. Live fully without distraction and with energized passion and tenderized compassion, knowing that you will often be distracted. In the twilight between light and dark is found each error, mistake, bend, and sin that provides grit and grist for the circular mill to turn its sacred wheel and move you along the highway to heaven.

The 3-D Mystery Painting

On my birthday, I received this email from a friend who had experienced a powerful visionary dream. She wrote:

> I had quite an amazing dream of you, dear Brad. It occurred on the dawn before Easter Sunday. You were a painter and a master teacher, dressed as a Renaissance man with his students in the fifteenth century. I watched you walk around a huge studio filled with light as you taught a class of twelve of us. Then suddenly you came to me and painted a portrait of Jesus, doing so by pushing your paintbrush

through the display of my laptop. The painting became a 3D figure, like a statue. It began to move around. Your brush went through the computer screen again and drops of blood started to fall from Jesus. As they fell the drops of blood turned to beautiful peony petals. Jesus became a sculpting that revolved in space, dropping blood that turned to flowers. You then said, "It's ready. You can now attach this portrayal of Jesus to your computer and send it as a link to others. Do so, please." I noticed a blonde-haired woman in the room who needed help, so I sent it to her. She started to weep while waiting for this important message. When she received the 3-D image, her face burst into a smile. It was such a vivid dream and I will never forget it.

Shortly after our friend's vision, I stumbled upon this quote by the famous mystic, Edgar Cayce. When asked about what should guide each person's life, he taught that

each soul should seek to attune its mind, its soul, its body-vibrations to what He, the Son of man, the Mother-God in Jesus the Christ, lived in the earth. Tune into that light, and it becomes *beautiful* in what you think, what you are, what you live![93]

In the vast mystery of the big room, the image and name of Jesus become multidimensional with endless forms, including that of a universal consciousness of love, the embodiment of the holiest light and spirit.

When Cayce was a small boy he went looking for a cow that had strayed from the family lot, and he accidentally ran into the famous evangelist Reverend Dwight L. Moody, who was alone kneeling in prayer by the riverbank. Cayce mustered the courage to approach him: "May I ask you a question, Mr. Moody, and you won't think I'm crazy, as so many seem to that I have asked this same question? You say you ask God's guidance, but did God ever speak to you?"[94] Reverend Moody shared a story about his own life to young Cayce in response:

> One day I was walking in a more humble section of that great city [London] when I noticed in front of me on a ledge a window box in which a geranium was blooming. I was attracted by its unusual color. As I approached it I heard a sweet, lovely voice singing, "Sweet Hour of Prayer." I stopped to listen, and after a bit felt impelled to climb the stairs to find the singer. At the head of the stairs there was an open door from which the song came. I peeped in, asking if I might join whoever was there. And I saw a poor, little lame girl, who said, "Oh, Mr. Moody, it's you. I knew God would answer my prayer and send you here. I read of you in one of our newspapers and have been praying for you to come to London for several weeks now." My meeting in London started right there in that little girl's room. I knew it was God who spoke to me. What channel He used, I don't know, but I heard a message from Him to go up to that child praying there for Light and for a message from me.[95]

Reverend Moody then said to the young Cayce, "So, Eddie, you may be assured that I do not think you foolish." Soon after this meeting, Cayce's formative mystical experiences began. He was surely comforted by his meeting with Moody in the years to come when he would be repeatedly accused and tried by other church members for heresy. Nothing, however, would ever stop him from speaking to God.

Do not hesitate to call upon the name of a holy one whose embodiment of love transcends all human laws and judgment. Allow such a captain to guide and direct your life. Do not worry whether others criticize you; only make sure the size of the room in which you stand is infinite and that your communication with God is direct. A multidimensional icon of Jesus has been reborn inside a mystery where drops of blood turn to flower petals, the beauty of which beckons you to come closer to hear its sacred song. We pray that you find joy and love in every sweet hour of prayer.

There Will Never Be Another You

Not long after the Joseph Hart vision, I had a dream of the jazz trumpeter Chet Baker. He appeared as a thousand-year-old man and his face looked like it was made of stone. Then I realized that I was becoming like that old and ancient man who could barely walk. He was in his living room with a younger wife and a group of students. He was sitting behind a piano and he sang a song to the class, "There Will Never Be Another You." Its lyrics follow:

> This is our last dance together
> Tonight soon will be long ago
> And in our moment of parting
> This is all I want you to know
> There will be many other nights like this
> And I'll be standing here with someone new
> There will be other songs to sing, another fall, another
>   spring
> But there will never be another you
> There will be other lips that I may kiss
> But they won't thrill me like yours used to do
> Yes, I may dream a million dreams
> But how can they come true if there will never, ever
> be another you?
> Yes, I may dream a million dreams
> But how can they come true if there will never, ever
> be another you?[96]

The dream of Chet Baker was interesting because he was playing the piano. Few people know that he was a pianist in addition to being a trumpeter and singer. We also didn't know this prior to the dream, and discovered there exists one album on which he plays the piano. The name of the album is *There Will Never Be Another You*.

There absolutely will never be another you. You are unique and everything about you is beautiful, including all you may think isn't beautiful. Let us never forget that every day is the last dance and that every moment is your last chance to be the only you that will ever exist. Know that you will sometimes have missteps, trips, and stumbles. Like a jazz musician, you must welcome each unanticipated outcome, including the occasional clunker note, as an opportunity to creatively embellish the ongoing melodic line of your life. As Miles Davis is said to have advised, "It's not the note you play that is the wrong note—it's the note you play afterward that makes it right or wrong." Learn to go past regarding any particular outcome as an error or mistake. Every blunder is an invitation to invent a subsequent action that makes it right in an altered way, doing so to improvise a creative life. In music, one note leads to another note with some surprising changes thrown in along the way; the same is true for the musical climb up the rope to God. Head to the biggest ballroom where there is enough room for every note, step, word, and action to beautifully contribute to the ongoing jazz of change. There you will find that past all dreams lies the moving truth that there will never, ever be another you.

Heavenly Sunshine: A Ticket to the Fast Lane

Brad had another dream several nights after visioning Chet Baker where he received a song he had never heard before. A voice told him it was a "ticket to the fast lane to heaven," meaning it was a strong rope to God. This time it was not Beethoven, Liszt, or Chet Baker. It was an old gospel tune sung by J. Robert Bradley, the favorite singer of both Martin Luther King, Jr. and gospel legend Mahalia Jackson. Its lyrics follow:

When our hearts are bound in sorrow
And it seems all help is gone
Jesus whispers do not falter
I will leave you not alone
Then somehow amidst my trials
How it is I cannot see
Then I hear a voice from heaven
Gently saying follow me

There is sunshine in the shadows
There is sunshine in the rain
There is sunshine in our sorrows
When our hearts are filled with pain
There is sunshine when we're burdened
There is sunshine when we pray
There is sunshine, heavenly sunshine
Blessed sunshine all the way

Let me recommend him to you
I have found no better friend
He is one who will not deceive you
But stay with you to the end
If you would have peace and comfort
Let his banner be unfurled
For he lifted rugged Calvary
And his name can save this old world

Sometimes my friends forsake me
And I'm tempted to despair
Then I think of my dear savior
To lay his head he had no where
Oh it pays to follow Jesus

Just to learn of him each day
And I'll guarantee you my brothers
You'll have sunshine all the way[97]

This song, composed by Lucie E. Campbell, the earliest African American woman gospel songwriter,[98] was so spiritually powerful that we repeatedly listened to it each day for the weeks and months that followed. It was like going to a spiritual gas station and constantly filling up with the highest octane fuel. "Heavenly Sunshine" also helped us administer healing power to others who were suffering from unfortunate life circumstances. This song made our ropes so strong that we thought we'd fly straight to heaven. Indeed, "Heavenly Sunshine" is a ticket to the spiritual fast lane and it shot us quickly up the rope.

Its lyrics are a return to the central teaching of Joseph Hart. When you are bound in sorrow, think all help is gone, and sink into despair after being forsaken, a voice says, "Follow me." If you accept this invitation and sincerely pray, the light from above arrives to bring heavenly sunshine to relieve your sorrow, pain, and burden. Here you find how Reverend Hart pointed to the highest mystery of spirituality: suffering offers you the choice to get on your knees and pray rather than try to will it away. In this submission to a greater divine love and wisdom, sunlight fills your darkness and brings soulful healing, sacred illumination, and ecstatic spiritual fire.

Receiving "Heavenly Sunshine" from the spiritual classroom also introduced us to its composer, Lucie E. Campbell, who during her time was called "The Mother of Gospel Music." Born in 1885, she became one of the greatest African American gospel composers. When Campbell was just nineteen she recruited a number of musicians on Beale Street in Memphis to form a musical group that evolved into a thousand-voice choir. The choir performed at the National Baptist Convention and

Campbell later became the convention's music director. In 1919 she published her first song, "Something Within," which has been recorded by numerous gospel stars and was sung by freedom riders during the civil rights movement. Her songs, with all their musical innovations, shaped the worship style of many black churches. Campbell's rhythms and soulful renditions saturate both church and secular music. Her introduction of gospel waltz time was later picked up by Ray Charles and also sung by the musicians she discovered, such as Marian Anderson, Thomas Dorsey, and J. Robert Bradley.[99] The more we learned about Lucie E. Campbell, including her pioneering social activism, the more we wanted to honor her life.

Campbell was no stranger to discrimination. She had to fight for her right to preach inside black congregations who insisted the role of preaching should be reserved for men. Lucie was a "prayer warrior" who believed in the power of prayer. She would spend hours in prayer and devotion. After teaching a Sunday school class on Easter, she was moved to write the hymn, "In the Upper Room with Jesus." It urges those in despair to head to "the upper room of our hearts to commune with our Lord."[100] It is dedicated to all those who have discovered the prayer way of climbing to the big room of holy mystery. Lucie Campbell's life was not about winning awards or achieving worldly fame. Few know her story today, but surely her life was pleasing to God. In the upper room of prayer she sang, "Touch, touch me Lord Jesus. With thy hand of mercy, make each throbbing heartbeat feel thy power divine."[101]

English mystic Julian of Norwich, another woman prayer warrior, taught that "[p]rayer fastens the soul to God and makes it one with his will, through the deep inward working of the Holy Spirit."[102] This is the main offering of prayer. It is not merely a matter of demonstrating religious belief. It is a major spiritual tool, mystical method, and holy secret. In prayer is found the practical means of establishing and strengthening your rope to God. The same can be said for singing holy songs, like "Heavenly Sunshine." Prayer and song remind us that even in very dark times, there is an ever present, pervading light that shines on everyone. Songs are a means of transport that can lift you out of difficult circumstances and deliver you to ecstatic joy. We repeat the chorus to this mystical ticket to the fast lane to heaven:

> There is sunshine in the shadows
> There is sunshine in the rain
> There is sunshine in our sorrows
> When our hearts are filled with pain
> There is sunshine when we're burdened
> There is sunshine when we pray
> There is sunshine, heavenly sunshine
> Blessed sunshine all the way

An Altar for Spiritual Cooking

Shortly after I received the song, "Heavenly Sunshine," Hillary had this vision:

> We were gathered for a Sacred Ecstatics intensive somewhere in the European countryside. Immediately next door to the gathering place was a very old Catholic monastery with a church made of stone. I wandered over there during the break with one of our friends, Nathalie. It was gently raining outside. As we walked along the side of the church, feeling refreshed by the raindrops, I noticed a small room with a vaulted ceiling that had been built in a gothic style. In the middle was an unusual altar that caught my attention. It was very simple and plain. Somehow I knew that it was where the monastery cooks went to pray. The altar consisted of three thick, stone steps with only enough space for one person to

kneel. There was a platform on top that held a large mortar and pestle. I was excited by this discovery and decided to climb the altar, kneel, and pray. In front of me I saw a window, a table with wooden kitchen tools, and a simple crucifix on the wall. I felt the rope to God tug on my heart as I prayed for a short while. Our friend, who had been watching, was happy with what transpired and we embraced before returning to the gathering next door. The next morning I sketched the altar I had seen in vision:

When Hillary lived at the Zen Center of Los Angeles, she had served for a time as the kitchen coordinator. In addition to cooking, she managed the rotation of other cooks and various kitchen-related tasks. As Hillary was taught, cooking is to be regarded as the embodiment of spiritual activity, being of no less importance than meditation, chanting, or prayer.[103] Hillary further comments on this teaching:

My time at the Zen Center of Los Angeles gave me the deep appreciation of cooking for others as a spiritual practice. Although "cooking your life" is a metaphor I first encountered in Zen, it took on a whole new meaning when I experienced how the phrase is used by the Kalahari Bushman doctors. In the Kalahari, "getting spiritually cooked" refers to being filled with *n/om*. It isn't so much an abstract metaphor as it is a description of what is experienced in the body during a dance. As some ecstatic Christians say, spiritual ecstasy feels like a "fire in the bones."

In a Zen monastery there is an altar in the kitchen where the cooks make prayers and offerings before each meal. In my vision, the altar for the cooks was not in the kitchen, but attached to the church. Making the shift to ecstatic spirituality means moving the kitchen into the main room of spiritual activity, the purpose of which is to be set on fire and get spiritually cooked. As Brad and I like to playfully say when introducing Sacred Ecstatics, "Welcome to God's kitchen, where you are the main course!"

It isn't lost on me that the mortar and pestle in my vision looked exactly like the bowl-shaped bells with strikers we used at the Zen Center, which I also was assigned to ring. Such is the mysterious morphing of forms inside First Creation, where kitchen altars move into worship halls, kitchen tools are also bells, and you are beckoned to climb the stairs of the altar and kneel before the holiest means of cooking your life.

Hillary Visions and Dances into the Bushman Women's Way

Soon after her vision of the altar Hillary woke up in the middle of the night strongly feeling her ropes to the Bushman doctors she had danced with in the Kalahari, especially the women I am closest to and had danced with for many years. She felt them so strongly that she reached over and began shaking me with her hands. We shook and sang together most of the night. The next morning Hillary remembered a vision she had a few years earlier of the Bushman women. It was right before our first visit there together:

> I had gone to sleep praying about the trip we had planned to the Kalahari. I was eager to go, and yet there had been many logistical barriers in the way. This, along with a dream Brad had recently had about discovering a black mamba snake outside his tent in the Kalahari, had filled me with doubt about whether the trip was a good idea. I prayed that God's will be done. That night I had one of my first strong visions.
>
> I dreamed we were in the Kalahari and three of the women doctors took me to a dance to show me an old man who they said was the strongest doctor in the Kalahari. We clapped and sang while we watched this old man dance. After the dance the scene changed, and the three women and I were in a restaurant booth. Brad was downstairs in another part of the restaurant with another man. They had left me alone with the women so we could talk further. N!ae Kxao, the strongest doctor, began telling me more about the old man we had watched dance. I realized that she was talking about her late husband, |Kunta Kxao, who Brad had danced with for many years.
>
> I recalled that Brad previously told me that

|Kunta had been much older than N!ae, and when she was a young woman she assisted him in the dances. After he passed away, he began visiting her in visions to give her nails of *n/om*. This is how N!ae became a very strong doctor.

As N!ae continued to tell me what a strong doctor |Kunta was, she became filled with the sacred vibration of *n/om* and its extraordinarily strong emotion. Suddenly she looked me straight in the eyes and held her clenched fists upright on either side of her face. She shouted with the strongest power in her voice: "I love him so much, I could crap him out!" When she said this, it shot a powerful blast of *n/om* right through me. I woke up with so much vibratory energy that I thought I would dance on the ceiling!

N!ae's statement might sound like a strange way to describe affection, but in the Kalahari, metaphors related to defecation take on a sacred connotation when expressed in the context of matters related to the spiritual energy of *n/om*. Her husband's initiatory vision involved |Kunta being thrown up the anus and intestine of a giraffe where he danced with the ancestors.[104] He regarded this as his most powerful and important vision. The anus and intestine are the areas of the body most closely associated with transformation and change, aspects of creation most highly valued in Bushman spirituality. Hillary's vision continues:

Just after N!ae shouted and gave me an incredible blast of *n/om*, a waiter came to the table. Brad had sent up an order of vanilla ice cream for us to enjoy, which the women promptly began devouring. The waiter also had something on his tray for me. It was a small iPod with headphones. I picked it up and put the headphones over my ears and heard a song. It was the country music hit "Just You and I," a duet sung by Eddie Rabbit and Crystal Gayle. Some of the lyrics follow:

Just you and I
Sharing our love together
And I know in time
We'll build the dreams we treasure
And we'll be all right, just you and I

And I remember our first embrace
That smile that was on your face
The promises that we made

Just you and I
We can entrust each other
With you in my life
They'll never be another
We'll be all right, just you and I

We made it, you and I[105]

Hillary woke up from that vision filled with joy, knowing that the love between N!ae and |Kunta is like the love we share for each other: it is romantic love but it is also *n/om* love. Our "first embrace" was a *n/om* hug. We did end up taking the trip to the Kahalari, and N!ae was delighted to hear about Hillary's vision. They celebrated that she was filled with many nails of *n/om* and was already a strong *n/om-kxao*, or Bushman doctor. When Hillary danced with the women, it was clear to everyone that she had stepped into her destiny. The ecstatic movements and sounds that have been kept alive for thousands of years in the Kalahari flowed through her body naturally and effortlessly, a true testimony to how spiritually cooked she had become. The Kalahari elders gave Hillary their approval and blessing to teach the Bushman way of dancing with God and sharing *n/om*. As an amusing side note, over the years I had often fantasized bringing ice cream to the Bushmen as a special treat. Hillary's visionary dream and her ecstatic presence in their dance filled us with gratitude for our deep, familial relationship with our Kalahari sisters and brothers.

God is a Vibration

When I lived with Ikuko Osumi Sensei in Setagaya, Japan, I had an unusual vision that shook the core of my being. I actually woke up worried that an earthquake was taking place as I was physically rocking back and forth on the bed.

> In the dream I was told that I would be taken to the beginning of time where I'd witness the birth of the universe. Rather than be given a vantage point from which to observe this origin, I was stretched out on a table. I wondered whether something would occur inside of me.
>
> Then it happened: I felt the whole universe take one breath and it was indistinguishable from my own. The universe and I had one cosmic breath together, one cycle of inhalation and exhalation. I learned that only one breath like this was necessary for the whole of creation because it somehow embraced all of time and was complete in and of itself. I was told that this singular breath, which is also the original pulse, rhythm, or vibration, brought the universe into being. All realities are vibrational and most importantly, God is the *original vibration* behind the breath of life.

I would later learn that Edgar Cayce had experienced a similar mystical realization that "vibration is that same energy, same power, ye call God."[106]

In the beginning was a singular vibration that gave rise to

never-ending echoes of its sound. Every subsequent vibration is a transform of the same original vibration—the creative force of the divine creator. You, too, consist of vibrational transforms of the original vibration. The pulsed rhythms of vibration provide the cohesive glue holding together (making whole) the parts of you, whether they are separate cells and organs, or distinct thoughts, emotions, and experiences. The highest vibrations are spiritual and they affect all vibrations below them. If you are spiritually attuned, this affects your whole physical, mental, and emotional wellbeing. Therefore all work that aims to raise vibrations to their utmost power must involve awakening an experience of divinity, which feels at once like the most encompassing love, the brightest light, the hottest fire, and the strongest vibration.

In this vision I was also taught the law of octaves, previously envisioned by Pythagoras, Nikola Tesla, and Charles Henry, among others. For example, a whole diatonic scale of musical notes comprises an octave. Starting at any note, it takes seven notes to return to that same note, the eighth note, which is now the beginning of the next higher scale. Each vibration on the musical scale interacts with all the other vibrations, making harmony possible when certain notes are combined. This structure of octaves is also found in the periodic table of elements. The elements are arranged in the order of increasing atomic weights where every eighth element is similar to the first. Over five thousand years ago the ancient Egyptians referred to the number "8" as the "sacred constant." This knowledge was extended by the Greeks, especially by Pythagoras, who is given credit for first noticing the law of octaves. He also elaborated the natural laws concerning the ratios behind harmony and created a whole cosmology based on eights. Pythagoras concluded that everything was music, even stone, which he called "frozen music." Tesla, following a vision of how the universe follows the law of octaves, was inspired to invent the alternating current generator. Finally, Srinivasa Ramanujan, the extraordinary mathematical genius from India who claimed to be given mathematical formula in dreams from his family goddess, Mahalakshmi of Namakkal, would later mathematically calculate the maximum number of dimensions there are. Not surprisingly the number he found was eight.

If you understand the relationship between notes in a musical scale, then you have all the fundamental understanding needed to appreciate the law of octaves. For instance, you must walk up or down the notes of one scale to reach another. There is a gap between each note so a leap must be made to move from one note to the next. At the same time, each note is in relationship to all the other notes. The tonality of each note marks a shift in sound and vibration (and mood and orientation). The Russian mystic Gurdjieff studied the law of octaves and concluded that there is no straight line in nature. Everything is always ascending and descending, as well as weakening or strengthening a vibration, and no matter where you begin, you will always end up turning in a circle. If you start in one direction, you end up in the other direction. This kind of consideration led him and others before and after him to conclude that the same law of octaves that applies to sound vibrations and music applies to all other properties of nature from light to heat, magnetism, and the whole range of human experience.

When applied to mysticism, we find that the spiritual climb traverses a ladder with eight steps or vibratory locales, done in a circular, rather than linear, trajectory so that going up eventually becomes going down and vice versa. This trajectory also applies to how we relate to the law of octaves. After a mystic gains any kind of understanding of the vibrational nature of reality, there arrives the risk of a subsequent verbal drift that extends theoretical postulation into abstract obfuscation and muddle. Clarity only returns when you are retuned and returned to the highest divine vibration. This attunement is best accomplished when you sing in an ecstatic way, allowing the highest vibrations to pour out of your voice. Like the Bushmen of the Kalahari, you sing to climb, aware that each step up and down the ladder is analogous to the degree of vibrational energy experienced in the body and expressed through song. The ladder or rope to God is a song and you must express its melodic line until you hit the strongest note, a vibration that is not something easily written about, but only heard and felt and realized when you are filled with its sacred pulse. At that moment you find the utmost vibration that is God, the mystical "eighth octave" that shall forever remain undefined.

One of our mentorship students, Shari, envisioned something special while she prayed. She saw a holy man, Pointer Warren—a former St. Vincent Shaker—holding a tall steel rod. He pounded it heavily against the concrete ground, producing a vibratory tone. I have seen the Guarani Indians do the same with hollowed bamboo tubes, producing vibrations and rhythms when they sing their ceremonial prayers. This pounding enables them to feel a strong vibration coming up from the ground into their feet at the same time that they feel it in their hands. When you enter First Creation, the mystical rope can at any time shift into a steel rod, a bamboo tube, a hollow pipe, or a human windpipe that hosts the vibratory sound that lifts you into high mystery.

When Jesus danced with the disciples at the last supper, they formed a circle and held hands while he stood in the middle and announced, "I would play on the pipes: dance all of you!" He later says, "The eight dances with us," referring to the Lord of the eight heavens and the eight "eldest Powers of the Pleroma, the fullness beyond the stars." He concludes, "To the universe belongs the dancer" (also translated as "The whole on high is a dance"). To understand his mystery teaching, you must dance. "He who danceth not knoweth not what is being done."[107] While some scholars like Andrew Harvey regard this as a metaphor (see his interview in *Play Life More Beautifully*[108]), ecstatics who physically enact and embody the metaphors of which they speak, especially the dancers of the Kalahari, would regard Jesus's invitation to dance as a literal directive. You must get off your sitting commentary and boogie to the tune of a holy pipe. Only then can the big vibration penetrate your whole being, leaving you inseparable from creation and its creator. The whole on high is a dance moved by a sacred vibration, with a song voiced by a singular encompassing breath!

Celebrating the Anointment

On February 18, 2015, Hillary went to a spiritual classroom that she reported as follows:

> Brad and I were attending a film showing. We were not in a theatre, but what seemed more like a hotel conference room. It was evening and people were filling the seats. A man and woman arrived that we greeted. Though we seemed friends with the couple in the dream, upon waking I realized I didn't recognize them. What struck me was that the man was wearing an astoundingly beautiful blazer made of very fine burgundy velvet with a hint of yellow and burgundy flowered silk peeking out from under the lapel. The color of the burgundy was rich and deep.
>
> The scene changed as daytime arrived. The same room transformed into a DMV (Department of Motor Vehicles) waiting room—the kind of place where you go to get your driver's license, license plate, and official ID. It had white linoleum floors, light blue walls, vertical plastic blinds, and rows of chairs everywhere. It was filled with St. Vincent Shakers, men and women (mostly women) sitting in chairs.

They were very serious and stoic, and told us that they were there to celebrate Brad's spiritual gifts from God. They also gave us a small key with a number on it. They began to sing a slow, deep, beautiful song. I do not recall their words, but was more struck by the sound of their voices, especially the women's voices. I saw Mother Ralph as she looks in one of the photos in Brad's book on the St. Vincent Shakers, wearing blue and with a very serious look on her face as she sang. Her voice bellowed a deep, booming, soothing bass tone that vibrated right through me. I was in awe of the sound of all their singing. The song at some point picked up pace as we were getting ready to leave and a man stood to dance. It was all in honor of celebrating Brad's gift. Everyone formed a line and danced toward the man who was leading the movements. There was an explosion of tremendous joy in the dancing and singing.

That morning Hillary tracked down Mother Ralph's daughter and emailed her a report about this vision. Denise responded immediately, writing that she had been looking for us:

These are beautiful words and an inspiration to you and Brad. It touches my heart. My mom was a true inspiration and she loved to sing. I miss her. We are trying very hard to keep her legacy moving. Thank you for reaching out to be my friend. My mom told me all about Brad. I have been looking for him for a very long time. I prayed and asked God for your connection. What are you going to do about the meaning of this beautiful dream?

Within hours Denise called us on the phone and we all personally met for the first time. She said that ten years ago her mother passed away. Before Mother Ralph died she had a vision of a tree that only had two breadfruits hanging on it and she saw each drop off. As they fell to the ground she was told they were Pointer Warren and Archbishop Pompey, two of Brad's spiritual teachers from St. Vincent. They passed away shortly after her dream. Mother Ralph then realized that she was also dying and called her daughter to her side. She said, "Brad has the light inside of him. Promise me that you will find him and go to him. He must share the light with others." Denise promised her, "I will find him and tell him that he must gather the people and minister to them."

It took Denise ten years to find us. Today after Hillary's dream we spoke with her for the first time. She said, "I have talked to others about you and promised my mother I would find you. I am so happy and grateful that we have finally met. I am supposed to tell you to gather the people and share your light. Now is the time. The people will come."

She then told us how she was first led to the St. Vincent mourning room where mystical education takes place. When her mother was alive in the past, Denise was asleep one night, but thought she was awake. Her mother came to her room in the vision and demanded, "Get out of bed and lie on the concrete floor." She didn't want to do it, but Mother Ralph continued, "Don't be disrespectful. Obey me and get on that floor!" When Denise lied down on the floor she heard her mother's deep voice shout into her ears, "Go be banned[m] by Pointer Roban!"

When she woke up, the sound of her mother's voice wouldn't stop. It vibrated deeply inside her whole body. Denise had never heard the name "Pointer Roban" before. When she reported the vision to her mother and another pastor, they said, "Look up his

---

[m] Here "banned" refers to having the mourning bands (pieces of cloth) bound around one's head in preparation for a prayer fast that seeks spiritual vision in what is called a "mourning ceremony."

name in the phone book. If there are many names like this, then choose one to call and when he answers, ask him if he is a churchman. Keep calling until you find him."

Denise found several men with this name in the phonebook and chose one. She called the number and a man answered. She asked, "Are you a churchman?" He replied, "Yes, Sister Denise, I am." Denise almost fainted and wondered if she was dreaming again. She immediately asked him, "How did you know my name?" He replied, "I dreamed you were coming. You had a very serious vision. It is time for you to light a candle." That was how Denise first went into the mourning ceremony, a prayer fast that sends you to the visionary spiritual classrooms.

By this time, Denise, Hillary, and I were shouting with joy on the phone. Denise told us her visions and shared her songs. Finally, she told us the meaning of Hillary's dream, confirming what we already knew. Among other things, she said this: "It is time for the people to gather. A spiritual flood is ready to begin. Your mission is like a fountain overflowing. Something has been opened. A spiritual flood is being released. The people will come to you. They may not know why they have come and gathered. Some will come because they dreamed you. They are coming."

In this way Denise completed her promise to her mother. She then said that she wanted to become even stronger with God and wanted to meet us in person so we could pray, sing, and be more in the spirit together. She also had this to tell others who seek the holy spirit: "Do not ask for any spiritual gift. Only pray that God's will be done. Do not pretend anything or else you block receiving what God intends to give you. The reason you must be honest is because if you act like you know something or own something spiritual, this becomes the barrier that blocks transmission of what is intended for you. You have a role that God will assign. You will only be happy if you accept what is given to you. There is no room for jealousy or envy. Only 'Thy will be done.'"

Bringing Forth the Teachings

On the evening of February 19, 2015, I was sent to an unusual visionary place located inside the earth.

> There I found a mystical library filled with rare and one-of-a-kind books on lost spiritual knowledge. I was told that they provide special teaching for tuning human beings to be in harmony with the divine. I was standing in awe as I beheld this extraordinary room when I suddenly heard a group of angry men shouting and making noise as they ran down a hall toward the library. I immediately was alerted that they were evil and armed with harmful intention — the agents of all that was dark and demonic — and they clearly wanted to kill me. Without thinking I grabbed the pile of books on the table directly in front of me and ran for my life. As I tried to escape I saw corridors going in all directions. It seemed that I went through every tunnel and passageway, like trying to get out of a complicated maze. I learned firsthand how all these twisted and misleading passageways had been built to entrap travelers who found themselves there. I was stunned by the complex design of the labyrinth, but I again heard the spiritual antagonists coming after me. I continued running and increased my speed and sense of desperation until I felt higher hands lead me on.
>
> Finally, I came to the surface where a gathering of people had assembled. Hillary asked what I was carrying and where I'd been. In all the commotion I had not looked to see what I had taken from the library. When I glanced down, I saw that I was holding the books we had authored on Sacred Ecstatics. In addition, there was a reel-to-reel tape

recording inside a box. When it was played, a voice said, "The flood shall be released." I started to weep as I heard music from St. Vincent.

I came back to myself with deep gratitude.

Here to Love

We are often sent to the spiritual classrooms to re-experience the teaching that no matter the question, love is always the answer. This love can never be fully grasped by mind; it must be deeply felt in order to be absorbed. During this time of intense visioning we had a client, a medical doctor from San Francisco, share with us an incredible story about a patient he once had who needed liver surgery. Following a successful operation, the man told the doctor, "Though everyone believes I will live, I know I won't leave this hospital." That night, at three o'clock in the morning, the patient had a vision and met an angel who told him the secret to life. It is this: *We are here to love.* He woke up in the hospital room and told his wife, who was there by his side, to tell the doctor what he learned in the dream and to give him a certain "Get Well" card that was on his table. The man then died.

The card that the man gave to his doctor friend had a painted image of angels that was attached to a piece of blue-colored cloth. Inside he found these words from Exodus 23:20: "Behold, I send an Angel before thee, to keep thee in the way, and to bring thee into the place which I have prepared." The doctor telling us this story said, "Today this is the holiest gift I own. I have it framed and it is on my medical office wall."

You are here to learn about divine love and how its mystical power can take you up the ladder, rope, staircase, or road to the big upper room. The angels are waiting to point and guide you, as are the saints, shamans, ministers, healers, and mystics of love. At the end of the ride, you return with these words: "So now faith, hope, and love abide, these three; but the greatest of these is love" (1 Corinthians 13:13). Past all miracles and illuminations of mind, the ultimate gift and homecoming awaits: immortal love. "Dear friends, let us love one another, for love comes from God. Everyone who loves has been born of God and knows God" (1 John 4:7). "And over all these virtues, put on love, which binds them together in perfect unity" (Colossians 3:14).

As Mahatma Gandhi found, "[w]here there is love there is life."[109] How can this be? e. e. cummings replies, "i carry your heart(i carry it in my heart)."[110] How? Antoine de Saint-Exupéry answers, "Love does not consist of gazing at each other, but in looking outward together in the same direction."[111] Do not forget Winnie the Pooh's reported advice when asked how to spell the word "love": "You don't spell it . . . you feel it" (A. A. Milne).[112] Why bother? Sophocles hints the reason, "One word Frees us of all the weight and pain of life: That word is love."[113] At the same time, "There is no intensity of love or feeling that does not involve the risk of crippling hurt. It is a duty to take this risk, to love and feel without defense or reserve" (William Burroughs).[114]

How are we to express love? Elizabeth Browning recalls, "Let me count the ways. I love thee to the depth and breadth and height My soul can reach."[115] We invite you to walk toward love, for there "lovers alone wear sunlight" (e. e. cummings).[116] When we meet the immortal beloved let us sing, "Yours is the light by which my spirit's born: — you are my sun, my moon, and all my stars" (e. e. cummings).[117] Do this knowing that, "This is love: to fly toward a secret sky, to cause a hundred veils to fall each moment. First to let go of life. Finally, to take a step without feet" (Rumi).[118] "Love is our true destiny. We do not find the meaning of life by ourselves alone — we find it with another" (Thomas Merton).[119]

"Down on the lake rosy reflections of celestial vapor appeared, and I said, 'God, I love you' and looked to the sky and really meant it. 'I have fallen in love with you, God. Take care of us all, one way or the other'" (Jack Kerouac).[120] And remember this, from W.B. Yeats:

> WHEN you are old and grey and full of sleep,
> And nodding by the fire, take down this book,
> And slowly read, and dream of the soft look
> Your eyes had once, and of their shadows deep;
>
> How many loved your moments of glad grace,
> And loved your beauty with love false or true,
> But one man loved the pilgrim soul in you,
> And loved the sorrows of your changing face;
>
> And bending down beside the glowing bars,
> Murmur, a little sadly, how Love fled
> And paced upon the mountains overhead
> And hid his face amid a crowd of stars.[121]

Receiving a Healing Doll

One night before Hillary went to sleep she felt the preciousness of the time that she and I have together in this life. She told God, "I know this work is about helping others. I am willing to serve you and offer myself wherever and with whomever you see fit. I do not have the wisdom to know what is best. Please take me, show me, and use me how you will." She spoke this prayer with a heart full of humility, surrendering herself to the Almighty.

Hillary had a spiritual journey that night.

> I envisioned that I was alone in the back seat of a car, waiting for something or someone, when I fell asleep and had a dream inside my dream. In this dream I was standing on a sidewalk outside an airport where there were many people standing around waiting to meet each other. My father came up to me and as I looked him straight in the eyes it seemed I had had this dream before but somehow didn't finish it. This

time I wanted to make sure that I held his gaze, remembering that if you want clarification about something in a vision, you must ask for it. I asked my father, "Do you have something for me?" He said yes, and then a nearby woman with long hair who was wearing purple came up to us. She handed me a small doll that was about six inches tall and made of wood and cloth. The wooden, carved head of the doll was painted black and white. It was the head of a dog with a white face—having a long white snout and long black ears. It looked like a piece of hand-made folk art that would please a child. The bottom half of the doll was covered in a purple skirt. I could not see the other end clearly, but was told by the woman that I could turn the skirt up and make the bottom half of the doll become the head, and vice versa.

My father and the woman told me that this was a gift to be used in helping and healing others. Upon hearing this I burst into tears. I then woke up from that vision and returned to my first dream, where I was still inside the car sleeping. While still in the dream, I wrote down every word on a yellow legal pad and drew the doll I had been given, thinking how important it was to show it to Brad.

The topsy-turvy doll most likely originated in the early nineteenth century on Southern plantations, and historians still argue over what they were supposed to symbolize. There are many conflicting ideas about the purpose they served, especially concerning relations among white and black people of the time. For example, it has been suggested that the dolls depicted a white woman on one side and a black woman on the other. A young girl could play with either side of the doll in the privacy of her home, but then flip it at any time to hide one side while publicly showing the other side. [122] Whatever the reason or reasons for its use, we can agree that such a doll enables its owner to flip back and forth between whatever ideas seem to conflict even as they coexist. Hillary's mystical doll has a dog's head and it is both black and white. Is the other side another dog or a human? Is it white, black, or multicolored? Perhaps it is the head of that which shall forever remain unseen. With her doll, multiple differences, contradictions, and paradoxes may cross the border between the seen and unseen, the known and unknown, and the human and not human—all partial sides in need of being made whole, all held inside a complexity of coexistence, ready to be turned as the changing requires.

When you go to the spiritual classrooms, there is no end to the kinds of spiritual gifts that can be received. You may acquire a new song, a dance, a doll, or be shown something that you need to find or make. All of these gifts strengthen your rope, bridge, and link to divine mystery. They are given to help you help others. Always remember that a dream may be held inside another dream as you, too, reside inside multiple rooms and existential spaces. To be a healer or spiritual teacher you must learn to host the topsy-turvy changing of experience, recognizing that one gift may hold another gift that is only revealed when you turn it upside down.

The Married Visions

I went to a spiritual classroom where an elder's voice directed me to go on a journey to find a special gift.

> The old man mentioned that there would be a sign marking the location where the treasure would be buried. I had to make my way through crowds of people who were caught in all kinds of worthless discussions—false teachings that inflated egos, specious arguments, and irritating sales pitches,

along with other distractions and obstacles that blocked the journey. It was quite a long ordeal, but I finally came to where the land ended, and there I faced a great ocean. At the shore, I realized I was in India because of the way the people looked and were dressed. They were bringing gifts, mostly gold and silver coins, and leaving them on the sandy beach. As I came closer to the ocean, I saw a clearly marked sign on the ground. It was the imprint of a single footprint. As I stared at it, a mysterious vibration was felt reverberating throughout my body. Underneath this imprinted foot was found spiritual treasure — a mystery that can only be received and shared through the highest stirring of emotion.

When I told Hillary about this spiritual vision, she said a Buddhist teacher previously told her that the Buddha was sometimes symbolized as a single footprint, a metaphor for "the path." We did some research and found that this was the oldest symbol in India for a guru or spiritual teacher, even before Buddha's time. Though these steps are usually found on stone or rock, in my vision it was made in the sand. Anyone standing on it was one step away from dissolving and becoming part of the vast sea of mystery.

Hillary then told me that she also had gone to a spiritual classroom that same night. Here's her story:

I was with Brad visiting what seemed like a small European village; a tour guide was showing us around. It was Wednesday evening and there were several small Catholic chapels that were holding an evening service. As we walked past them, I looked in and noticed the services were sparsely attended by mostly elderly women. This made me feel a bit sad to see that an interest in spiritual worship was waning.

We came to the doorway of one of the small chapels—it looked like a simple classroom with rows of chairs. The service had just ended and the priest was packing up his things. A few people were still chatting and also gathering their things to leave. I noticed that the priest had drawn a large symbol on the blackboard in colored chalk. I assumed that it must be some kind of special religious holy day in the Catholic tradition. The image was a large rendering of a giant pinecone, drawn the way it would look if it were done in stained glass with many bright colors of red, pink, green, and yellow. There was an elderly woman standing in front of the blackboard looking at the symbol. She had a long stick and proceeded to use it to count the number of layers on the image from the top down. I heard a voice say that she was planning to make the image on a quilt. Then I woke up.

When Hillary shared her vision with me, we realized that we had experienced two "married visions," each belonging to the other. Both the foot imprint on the sand and the pinecone in the chapel lead to profound spiritual treasure. The pinecone has historically served as a symbol of spiritual enlightenment, the illumined dissolve into the whole of divine mystery. Here the rising mystical fire climbs all the steps of the holy spine until it reaches the top and awakens spiritual vision of the divine light. This climb corresponds to the Egyptian Staff of Osiris with its pair of intertwined snakes moving upward to make contact at a pinecone, sometimes regarded as the mystical third eye held in the pineal gland. Depictions of Hindu deities also often include portrayals of pinecones. The Greek god Dionysus, later known as Bacchus to the Romans, had a fennel staff topped with a pinecone, and a pinecone is found on top of the sacred staff carried by the Pope. Given the dream setting in which Hillary witnessed the pinecone, we direct you to this scripture from Hosea (14:8):

> O Ephraim, what more have I to do with idols?
> I will answer him and care for him.
> I am like a green pine tree;
> your fruitfulness comes from me.

The green pine tree or evergreen in Semitic symbolism is regarded as an image of spiritual receptivity and a divinely nourished life. A pine tree is green and full of life, provides shelter, and makes a wood that can endure the stress of changing weather. As a spiritual symbol the pinecone and its tree remind us that God's love is ever-lifegiving, ever-growing, everlasting, and evergreen. The pinecone calls us to keep pining for the ultimate mystery that can only be reached at the edge of the vast sea. Past all distracting temptation and tangential speculation, there is a single footprint that marks the way. Underneath it is found a spiritual treasure that, meant for the heart, is beyond words.

In the Garden

I dreamed that Hillary and I took our mentorship students to my paternal grandparent's former house at 2101 North Second Street in St. Joseph, Missouri. It was the parsonage I fondly remember visiting as a young boy. We invited each student to stand outside the house and look through the kitchen window. There they saw my grandmother's refrigerator and stove.

The next night I had another dream and saw the rope to God as large as I have ever seen it. It was large enough to hold a white wooden country church that was high in the sky, along with clouds that sheltered many angels and luminous, mysterious forces. The rope intermittently flashed with lightning and was filled with thunderous praise and song. Literally, an amazing shower of blessings took place and I was filled with spiritual electricity, rhythm, and music.

Several days after these dreams, I went to a spiritual classroom where the sacred emotion was so strong that I wept for over an hour after I woke up. I was sent again to my paternal grandmother's kitchen. I called her "Doe," a name I gave her as a child because she reminded me of a sweet and kind female deer. I called her this throughout her life.

> I sat at Doe's kitchen table facing her stove with Hillary on one side and my mother on the other side. My grandfather was also present, standing and looking over us at the end of the table. Without saying a word, Doe proceeded to chop many vegetables and place them in a large, clear plastic bag that was about two feet tall. With a glow in her eyes, she sat this bag of chopped vegetables on the middle of the table directly in front of me.
>
> As I stared into the vegetables of many shapes, sizes, and colors, I was surprised to see that they had somehow fallen together in such a way that musical notes were created. Suddenly a keyboard appeared on the table and I began playing this unique musical score. My family started to sing along and as the music continued, other relatives arrived in the kitchen, including my sister and, finally, my father. They floated into the room through the ceiling near my grandfather. Soon everyone was singing the old hymn, "In the Garden," a favorite of my grandmother. As my emotions grew, the vegetable notes disappeared and I was unable to play the keyboard anymore. I could only sing. My whole family sang in unison and the sacred emotion was so strong that I wept from the depths of my soul.

I woke up and was still inside the song, feeling its verse as a fire in my soul:

I come to the garden alone,
While the dew is still on the roses,
And the voice I hear falling on my ear
The Son of God discloses.

And He walks with me, and He talks with me,
And He tells me I am His own;
And the joy we share as we tarry there,
None other has ever known.

He speaks, and the sound of His voice
Is so sweet the birds hush their singing,
And the melody that He gave to me
Within my heart is ringing.[123]

The composer of this song, C. Austin Miles (1868–1946), was a pharmacist and amateur photographer. One day in 1912 in the month of March, while in his darkroom waiting for film to develop, Miles had a profound spiritual experience in which he saw an incredible vision of Mary Magdalene visiting the empty tomb of Jesus. He saw her leave the tomb and walk into a garden where she met the master and heard him speak her name. When Miles came to himself his "nerves were vibrating and his muscles tense";[124] and the words to a new song were filling his mind and heart. He quickly wrote out the lyrics to "In The Garden" and later that evening composed the musical score. The song was published that same year and became a theme song of the Billy Sunday evangelistic crusades. After this experience Miles left his profession of pharmacy and became a hymn writer.

We shared this song with our mentorship students and they, too, were moved by its ability to spiritually empower their lives. The particular recording of the song that we like to share with others is the version sung by John McNeil, the pianist, composer, and arranger for the great gospel singer, Albertina Walker. It became one of the strongest threads in our rope to God.

Vættir

After the vision in Doe's kitchen, I was taken to a spiritual classroom and given an extraordinarily erudite lecture by a mystical master teacher. I was shown how there are always different but simultaneously occurring realities. Each reality is associated with a particular degree of spiritual temperature and existential room size; it is your spiritual temperature and the breadth of the space you occupy that determine the reality you experience. However, all realities—with their diverse temperature degrees and varying sizes—occur simultaneously. It is you who keeps moving and changing, and this influences what room and reality you experience. Inside the spiritual fire you experience reality as an indivisible, whole unity. When you spiritually cool down, the whole disassembles and you once again experience its differentiated partial forms. However, as you ascend and descend the rope to the sacred fire and move back and forth between small rooms and big rooms, all temperatures, rooms, and realities simultaneously remain.

Following this lecture, I was taken to an even higher classroom, a vast chamber where a voice of authoritative wisdom announced, "I will show you your destination, where you are to go. This will be revealed by one single word, a clue that will leave no ambiguity as to what it indicates. It will not only name where you need to be; it will also answer many other questions at the same time." A word was then projected onto a screen as I heard the voice say it out loud. I recall thinking that the word looked both familiar and unfamiliar at the same time. I felt spiritual energy pulse through me.

When I woke up and returned to myself, I repeated the word often to make sure I would not forget it. I did not get up to write it down because it seemed easy to remember. The next morning, I woke up and was startled because I could not be sure how the word was spelled. Was it "vattir" or "vettir"? The actual word was "vættir," an Old Norse word for spirit. *Vættir* refers to all spirits generally, as well as the differentiated nature spirits across many different realms, including the spirits of the forest, spirits of the lakes, spirits of the sea, elves, dwarves, giants, and gods. These spirits can intermingle and even marry one another or human beings. They may be a particular spirit or a whole family of spirits. Each spirit individual, family, or clan is capable of helping or harming, which is why the carved dragons on the Viking long ships were removed whenever new land was approached so the other spirits would not be provoked.

To understand how *vættir* is simultaneously the name of all spirits as well as the name of different spirits requires grasping the lesson I received in the visionary lecture. In the midst of strong ecstatic experience when the spiritual temperature is high and the existential room size is vast, *vættir* is experienced as an indivisible whole. You are in relationship to the greatest, singular source of all spiritual mystery. When the spiritual temperature drops and language and thought again become primary, you experience the way spirit (*vættir*) comes in many forms and moods, from helpful to harmful, wise to tricky, and everything in between.

When people only relate to spirits in cold temperatures, they tend to easily get caught up in fighting, extracting, or harnessing them to affect particular outcomes. Over everything else, aim for a strong relationship with the highest source. Avoid gambling and taking an unnecessary risk with anything less. The higher the spirit, the higher you can be lifted. The lower the spirit, the lower you can be lowered. Go for the highest power and don't be sidetracked by any lower derivatives that reside in the cold.

For example, we have sometimes been called to visit homes where someone is regarded as being possessed by an entity or demonic force. Over the years Hillary and I have learned that if a spirit causes someone trouble, it is better to not fight it. This only makes the spirit stronger and more determined to maintain its presence in an interaction with you. (The same is also true of any psychological symptom.) We never try to extract the spirit or in any way contribute to maintaining its presence by calling out its name or singling it out, either to befriend it or exorcize it. Instead, we aim to make the room bigger and the spiritual temperature hotter so that all beings and spirits at all levels are invited to take their appropriate place. Paradoxically, if you make more room for the unwanted spirit, it will be less troubling and may even become an ally under the right circumstances. As always, the problem with any problem is that the existential space is not vast enough. Make the room larger and all things considered can find their way home in the whole ecology.

Practically speaking, we make the rhythms and sing the songs that take us into the strongest light and invite everyone else present — person and spirit alike — to join us. In other words, we get everyone back in line with the vertical, straight rope to God. Here all differentiated spirits and souls, whether regarded as good or bad, are invited back to the source from which they came. In this welcomed entry to the big room and spiritual heat, any unwanted presences are integrated in a resourceful way. Again, if you go to war with spirits in a small cold room, they become further inflated and empowered as an antagonistic presence that becomes even more fractured from the divine whole. Exclusion almost always answers with a louder cry for inclusion!

Consider how ghosts and troublesome spirits are often accompanied by cold blasts of air. You need to get everyone — every spirit and person involved — to the hotter and more expansive spiritual room, coming together under the sky of the

Creator of all creation. As the master teacher taught in my vision, there are multiple simultaneously occurring realities. It is futile to argue or debate over which one is more "real." An unwanted spirit is troubling only in a certain room size and temperature. In an equally valid reality where the temperature is hotter and the room bigger, the same spirit is a resource or gift. Like the topsy-turvy doll in Hillary's dream, when things are turned one way, the other side remains though it is hidden from view. When all souls meet in the big room, everything is free to keep turning, flipping, changing, and expressing any aspect of the everlasting spiritual truth. Any lost, confused, and upset spirit only mirrors the same agony as the person with whom it is in relationship. Both need to be cooked in the big room where they are dissolved in the greater unity of God's love.

And the Music Floweth from Me

I went to a visionary classroom and heard these words spoken: "He reacheth down and toucheth my head and the music floweth from me; without His touch I could not sing two notes." Scripture and song then poured through me that included these teachings of old: "And so it was, whenever the spirit from God was upon Saul, that David would take a harp and play it with his hand. Then Saul would become refreshed and well, and the distressing spirit would depart from him" (1 Samuel 16:23). "And be not drunk with wine, wherein is excess; but be filled with the Spirit; Speaking to yourselves in psalms and hymns and spiritual songs, singing and making melody in your heart to the Lord" (Ephesians 5:18-19). "It came to pass, as the trumpeters and singers were as one, to make one sound to be heard in praising and thanking the Lord; and when they lifted up their voice with the trumpets and cymbals and instruments of music, and praised the Lord, saying, For he is good; for his mercy endureth for ever: that then the house was filled with a cloud, even the house of the Lord; So that the priests could not stand to minister by reason of the cloud: for the glory of the Lord had filled the house of God" (2 Chronicles 5:13-14).

Ecstatics from all traditions recognize the truth in the words I heard spoken. When you are directly touched by holiness, song flows out of you in the most powerful way. It is unlike any other kind of singing or instrumental performance you will ever experience. Only by the holy touch of mystical anointment does this kind of soulful, spiritually cooked music pour forth. Amidst this sound you are found inside the presence of God, the greatest music-maker in the universe.

Have Thine Own Way, Lord

I was sent to another spiritual classroom where a holy fork appeared in the sky and came down to feed me a delicious slice of cake, a sweet treat I like very much. I woke up to notice that my jaws were moving, like I was actually eating this heavenly dessert. As I was infused with a powerful holy current, I heard a voice say, "There is more than enough to share with everyone." If you are spiritually hungry, know that someone is waiting to feed you. The divine is ready to satisfy your deepest hunger with the most delicious offering and will provide enough for you to share with others.

The following night I spiritually traveled again and found myself standing in a large room holding many robes in my hands. I was holding at least fifty robes, if not more. I could only keep my eyes on the ceiling as I heard these words spoken, "Is the ceiling high enough? The robes must not touch the ground." I didn't look at the robes, the walls, or the floor. My gaze stayed upon the ceiling, wondering if it was high enough. I walked out of the room to a smaller room with a low ceiling. I heard again, "Is the ceiling high enough? The robes must not touch the ground."

The sound of an old hymn began to be sung by a gathering of people. It was the song I heard when fed cake by the holy fork. Now it was heard so strongly that it made me tremble even more. It also made the room bigger and the ceiling higher. Here are the beginning lyrics: "Have Thine own way, Lord! Have Thine own way! Thou art the Potter, I am the clay. Mold me and make me after Thy will . . ." With this song in my heart, I prayed and saw the rope to God. Its diameter was large enough for me to stand fully inside it. I looked up and saw all the way to heaven. Its luminosity and power were beyond measure and no words could begin to depict its immensity.

The End is the Beginning of Extreme Love

In a vision, Hillary and I were sitting in the back of an airplane. We were the only passengers on board and, strangely, the pilot was seated next to us in the back of the plane. He was dressed in a pilot's uniform, but was sitting in a lotus position with bare feet. The interior of the plane was somewhat like a bus in that you could see out a large window in the front of the plane. We were circling a channel of water to get ready for a landing when I noticed that the plane seemed too low. We were approaching a large ship and it became clear that we were going to crash into it. In a split second I had to decide whether to tell Hillary so that we would face this horrific ending together.

Instead of pointing out what seemed to be an inevitable catastrophe, I spontaneously turned and looked into her eyes. With all the life force in me I said, "I love you, Hillary." I had never expressed anything so deeply before in my entire life and she felt it. To our surprise we started to mysteriously dissolve into one another. As we felt this extreme love, our bodies transformed into floating sand-like particles that shone like tiny twinkling stars. We had no physical form; there was only a uniform mix of these floating particles — thousands of them — that gracefully danced while suspended in the air.

There was no awareness of the crash — no explosion, no noise, and no suffering. Instead, a holy fire lit the sky while we were both the tiniest particles on earth and the largest stars in the cosmos. In this embrace of opposites was found the greatest gift of joy — the realized embodiment of eternal love. The holy ships, planes, buses, and other means of spiritual transport are ready to take you into the holy water. Underneath is found the deepest place of the soul. Prepare to voice the love that conquers all and fly among the stars. This life is so brief, a mere moment. In the instant that you realize that it truly has an ending, choose to embrace what is eternal — everlasting love.

It Is Time to Correct History

The next night in a dream I heard a voice say, "Immediately go to the airport and fly to London. Do not wait. Go now." Hillary and I had no time to pack or get ready as the voice continued to insist that we head for the airport. We obeyed and on the way we realized that we had no tickets, but then we assured each other that we could purchase them at the airport. When we arrived, the airport lines were too long to get a ticket and catch the next flight. The voice replied, "Purchase it on the Internet." We did this and proceeded to successfully board the plane.

In the next scene, we were transported to a unique spiritual classroom. We were not in a city, but in the countryside. It was a place that looked like the landscape where I grew up as a child and it felt like home. There were hills and woods filled with tall trees. As we drove along a narrow country road, we saw a place on the right side of the road where we parked. The road ended there; immediately in front of us we beheld the most beautifully illumined pathway, bordered by tall trees on each side. It was a truly enchanting sight.

We walked down that path. There were no steps and no markers of any kind. The ground below was simply an old flat footpath that had not been traversed in a long time. At the end of the trail was an entry to a clearing. As soon as we went past where the tall trees and path ended, there stood a single ancient and majestic oak tree. It served as the backdrop for a small outside stage whose floor and benches were made of earth. An amphitheatre had been carved into the hill in front of the tree.

It felt like this place had been empty for a long time. This forgotten amphitheatre in the woods was a place that I experienced as both familiar and unfamiliar. As we examined this sacred place, my former teacher of cybernetics and systemic thinking, Gregory Bateson, entered the stage. He spoke with a serious tone and in his heavy British accent delivered these words: "You need to correct history. It is wrong."

Upon hearing this, both Hillary and I had the same thought. We didn't speak but wanted to say, "Gregory, we already did that. We did our best to straighten out the muddles that systems thinking, psychotherapy, and cybernetics had gotten itself into." Bateson, now unseen and only a voice, spoke again: "History is wrong. It is up to you to set it right." Hillary was the first to realize that Bateson was talking about more than the science of cybernetics and the profession of psychotherapy. He was talking about the whole of history itself, or at least something larger than we had at first assumed.

In that moment, we realized we were standing at an ancient and important classroom. It exists at the base of the tree of life, the tree of ancient wisdom and knowledge. There we all have a mission: to correct history, to get something right that has been misunderstood, misrepresented, and misdirected over all these years. In this theatre, forgotten teaching and performance wait to rise again.

Hillary's High Anointment

In an extraordinary vision, Hillary and I arrived at a retreat center in the woods to conduct our Sacred Ecstatics mentorship intensive.

The center was comprised of many buildings, including a theatre, a chapel, assorted lodging quarters, and a main hall. We entered the main room with a high ceiling and saw that students were arriving and milling about. I noticed that the wall on my right had a shelf with books on it. Hillary noticed with dismay that there was dust all over the room, especially on those books. She then started cleaning, sweeping the dirt away like a dedicated Zen practitioner. As Hillary cleaned the shelf and books with a rag, I noticed that she began to shrink with each swipe. She became smaller and smaller until she was actually crawling on the shelf as a tiny being, one the size of a fairy.

At the moment when she almost disappeared, a miraculous transformation began. She and I started ecstatically shaking together. At first, when she was tiny, I had to hold her and shake her in my hands. I did so until the energy became so intense that a loud sound took place, accompanied by an incredible metamorphosis: Hillary's outer skin appeared as a cocoon, which she then broke through like the birth of a butterfly. When she came out, she was larger in size. We kept shaking and the same process took place all over again. Hillary came out of one cocoon after another, repeatedly rebirthing, each time getting larger and more illumined. The first cocoon looked like paper and was followed by a covering of delicate tissue; with each emergence the cocoon changed its materiality until finally it was made of golden threads woven into a majestic cloth. When she finished all these metamorphoses, she was shining like the sun. Rays of light came out of her eyes and her whole body was extraordinarily luminous.

Hillary was so full of life force that the walls of the building vaporized. We were now standing inside a very large area without walls, as if floating in space. Suddenly a group of mystical beings arrived and two of them stepped forward. One appeared to be some kind of ambassador or representative of the many African ways of spirituality and healing, made apparent by his attire and how he spoke. He was so spiritually powerful that you did not want to look directly into his eyes for too long. The other man was introduced as "the original Taoist master," who presided over all caretakers of its many lineages. He walked in a way that looked like he was gliding over the ground. They both proceeded to carefully examine Hillary, asking her to sing, dance, and respond to other requests and questions. What had taken place with Hillary had set off some kind of alarm or signal in the cosmos and these ancestral guardians were sent to check out what was happening.

I was surprised to see that the countenance of these mystical officials soon radically changed. When they arrived they looked stern and were clearly there to carefully evaluate what was taking place. As Hillary was tested, however, their facial expression and gestures transformed. They were delighted with her responses and soon began celebrating what they beheld, shouting and making other movements to show their enthusiastic approval. This went on for a long time—an audition or final exam of the most thorough kind. At the end, the masters who had come from another realm encircled us, including those who had been standing in the background witnessing the ordeal. The Taoist man in charge gave a speech, saying he and the elders were pleased to announce their official confirmation that Hillary was "completely spiritually cooked." He then added, "Hillary Keeney is now a master." I was so proud of her that I began to weep. I knew it was true because I had witnessed her metamorphosis and felt her powerful vibration. The other elder masters approached her one by one to congratulate her, saying, "Welcome, you are now one of us." Before they left, the Taoist who served as the head of the investigation said, "You will forever take your place with us. You are ready to fulfill your mission without fear or concern. You have all that you need. Whatever else is needed will come when it is time for it to arrive."

A mystical fog then entered the room, and with it came a gathering of even more elders from cultures throughout the world. We were told that these were all the saints, shamans, healers, and spiritual teachers who had ever walked the earth. Each had previously received the same evaluation given to Hillary, as it is done to everyone who achieves mastery to perform a spiritual anointment. After they joined the circle, they began clapping their hands as the Taoist elder pointed to an empty seat. It was for Hillary. That was the moment she took her place in the room where the old ones reside. There, with thunderous applause, the elders proclaimed that Hillary had become a master spiritual teacher.

When I told Hillary the vision, she wept. Although she was very moved, she was also shy about it. She didn't want me to tell anyone else that it took place. I teased her saying, "Shall we shake you some more so you are big enough to handle the truth of your place in the world?" She then agreed that I could report it to the class, but I could only report a scaled-down version. I then knew that Hillary would never stop sweeping the floor and cleaning the dust off the shelf and books. I also knew that she would never be able to stop the changing that led her to sit in the chair of spiritual authority for teaching these lessons.

Entering the Kalahari Dream Time

After Hillary's high anointment, an extraordinary experience took place around the fire on a Saturday evening at the COD Ranch in Oracle, Arizona (this was an actual occurrence and not a vision). We were with our mentorship class following a long intensive together when we suddenly fell under the spell of a Kalahari *n/om* dance. It was every bit as strong and authentic as any dance I ever experienced in Africa. Here's a recap of what took place:

We were standing outside around a fire, talking and, especially, laughing. The conversation turned toward the Bushmen and the humor escalated, even getting a bit raunchy just like it does in the Kalahari. I announced that I sincerely wished he could fly everyone to the Kalahari right that moment and enter a Bushman dance. We later found out that either just before or after that declaration (we're not sure of the temporal order here), Berni, one of the mentorship students, saw a falling star and privately wished that he would receive *n/om*. He then followed his wish with the expansive prayer, "Thy Will Be Done."

I immediately felt a rope pull me toward Berni. To my surprise, I released a Bushman arrow of *n/om* into Berni's heart. In the classic *n/om-kxaosi* manner, I spontaneously let out the shrieking sound associated with the transmission of *n/om*. I was immediately experientially transported to the Kalahari and felt myself inside an actual dance. The door to the mystical Kalahari had been opened.

In the midst of Berni's receiving an arrow of *n/om*, Hillary started singing my most important *n/om* song. Her voice and mannerisms were expressed with a fully congruent Kalahari form. Other people began to clap and sing along. Suddenly we were all standing in the mystical Kalahari, a spiritual place not demarcated by geographical borders but found by entering the open door to the vast spiritual universe.

I felt many of the Bushman elders—men and women from my past and present—enter my body. More accurately, their dances were embodied and brought forth inside the circle. Arrows of *n/om* were flying everywhere, accompanied by more piercing shrieks. Hillary also felt the Bushman ancestors present and enter her voice and body. We were both surprised that the whole group quickly became like a Bushman community as we sang and clapped together. People formed a circle around Hillary and I, who danced in and out of the fire, sometimes putting our hands on other people. We became a mystical Bushman tribe that night under the stars.

The experience was so profound that the next morning it was the only thing people could talk about—it was hard to believe it actually took place. This remarkable experience was granted as a teaching to everyone, those present and not present. The spiritual power was so strong that staff members of the ranch reported seeing what they thought were ghosts in their rooms during the dance. The ancestors came down that night and danced with us. A man who had spent decades being the close helper of a traditional Lakota *Yuwipi* and Sundance medicine man later said it was the strongest ceremony he had ever witnessed. Hillary and I both felt that neither the mentorship program nor the world could ever be the same after it took place. We remain struck by this mystery ever since that night and have not quite left the mystical Kalahari.

In vision, I was told that history needed to be corrected. In other words, ancient truths need to be dusted off and resuscitated through re-entry into the changing of First Creation. Spiritual truth can become polluted, corrupted, reversed, or lost unless it is continuously enacted and embodied inside the spiritual fire. Let us say that Sacred Ecstatics is a new experiment in bringing life to old wisdom. It taps into the practical know-how behind the lineages that found their way to the home of the force behind creation—also called sacred ground, the vast sea, the sky village, earth as it is in heaven, and the big room. We welcome the arrival of this constantly changing re-emergence of creation. We never know what ceremonial forms, songs, or dances will come forth, but we put our trust in the singular divine rope that guides us. When we sincerely gather to ecstatically sing, dance, and climb the rope to God, as we did that night under the Arizona sky, the singing and dancing ancestors from the Kalahari and beyond rejoice and celebrate in kind. This is how ecstatic ceremony brings heaven and earth together, with those above and those below each reaching for one another as we all reach for the infinite divine.

The Chrysler Imperial

Shortly after the Kalahari dance in Arizona I was taken in vision to my grandparents' house where my grandmother, Doe, was waiting for me.

> We spent the evening talking about many things in her living room and I was both happy and sad because I knew I might never see her in this way again. She told me that when I got up in the morning she'd still be asleep, but that I should not wait for her to awaken. She then surprised me by gifting me with a car—a 1960 Chrysler Imperial that my grandparents had always dreamed of owning. "When you get up in the morning, drive this car home. You will find it is a very special car." We hugged and I told her how much I love her. I went to sleep and when I woke up, I followed her instruction and started to drive that car home.
>
> I was then suddenly struck by the realization that she had passed on. I was so overcome with grief that I thought I wouldn't be able to breathe again. I began

sobbing with tears and started to wake myself up. As I continued to weep, I found I could not quite fully wake up. I was suspended between the dream and being awake.

In this moment I recalled the last years of her actual life. In her nineties she began to lose her memory and I was amazed at how this enabled her to live totally in the present. I made a video for her with me sitting at the piano and playing her favorite hymns. I would pause to talk to her as if we were having a conversation and allow a few seconds to pass as if I was listening to her say something in return. I would then sing her a hymn. The whole video was like this, alternating between conversation and song.

It became a family source of humor that she spent the last years of her life watching this video all the time. She would get up in the morning and sit in front of the television until a meal was served, watching the video over and over again. She watched it each time as if it was the first time, remembering all the songs and the things I spoke to her about. She spent the last years of her life singing her favorite hymns with me.

As I remembered this, a voice pointed out that without knowing it I had given her a means of spiritual transport that enabled her to journey from her stuck situation to being fully awake and alive, traveling on the melodic lines of holy songs. I was brought to my knees with longing, loving, and gratitude as I realized she had just gifted me in a similar way. She had given me a spiritual means of transportation—the visionary car that was now parked outside our home.

The voice continued, "Take that car out for a drive. It can take you anywhere, including back to your grandmother." At first I didn't want to do this because I thought I was almost awake and I have an aversion to daydreaming; I tend to not trust too much con-sciousness inside my dreams. The voice replied, "Don't worry about that. This car will take you somewhere and your mind has nothing to do with it." That startled me, so I went to that Chrysler and turned the keys. I started heading to my grandmother's house.

The trip was vivid as I passed small towns, buildings, houses, and trees along the way. This was not a blurry, fast ride, but a trip that went slow enough to notice the details. As I entered the city of St. Joseph, Missouri, where they lived, I passed the old Pony Express statue, the old Indian Chief Chili stand, and all the old haunts of my childhood. Up the hill I went, passing the public library, and then turning left and down a few blocks to where their house stood. I parked where we used to leave the car and walked up the back stairs. Doe opened the door that was the entry to her kitchen.

We sat down at her table and started to sing her favorite song together. Tears were falling down my face when a voice said, "You can travel anywhere with this car." At that moment, the place in the ceiling near the back door opened and I looked up and saw a ray of light that seemed to stretch to heaven. Before I knew it, I was in the Chrysler driving along the beam of light. Like the child I had once been in that room many years ago, I said to myself, "I am flying faster than a speeding bullet!"

The voice asked, "Where would you like to go?" I replied, "I want to see my grandmother one more time." I was suddenly shot in space to a place that I knew was heaven. There was a choir singing in a church and I had no doubt she'd be there. I got out of the car and found her singing in the first row of the choir like she always did. I then thought that I wanted to see my grandfather. I trembled when I saw that he was sitting in a throne on the right side of God. He was pleased that I had come, but he remained where he was with a strong and happy countenance, allowing me to see that this was where he belonged. I used to see him this way when he was a country preacher. His chair was like a throne that was situated near the pulpit. Now he was back in church, this time the holiest of churches, and my grandmother was in the choir.

I asked out loud where Pointer Warren, Mother Ralph, Archbishop Pompey, and the other elders from St. Vincent were and the voice said, "They are in the mourning room." I was shown how they were praying in a celestial mourning room, doing so as other seekers on earth were also mourning. In that moment I was shown that whatever spiritual role you had on earth is continued in the heavenly plane. This time, however, you are the complement, or other side of someone reaching up from below. For every spiritual mourner and seeker of vision, someone in the heavens is also mourning and seeking vision with you. The singing on earth is matched by the singing in heaven. The same is true for teaching and preaching and all spiritual activity. In this way both ends of the rope are brought together. Heaven is brought into earth and earth into heaven as both sides reach for one another. I marveled at how all of this spiritually works and could not wait to tell Hillary.

I hopped in my car and bolted back to the earthly plane where I told Hillary to jump into the car. I drove her to heaven. I took her first to meet my grandmother. Doe was still singing but this time she stared at Hillary and gave her all her attention. I could see Doe light up with delight as she said, "Hillary is purely sincere and true. I am so happy for you." I then took Hillary to meet my grandfather and all my spiritual elders who welcomed and celebrated her with song and praise.

I was then handed a spiritual gift from my grandparents. It was a small case and when I opened it, I found a pair of spiritual tweezers inside. I was told it was for removing splinters and thorns. At first I was confused; then, I remembered that Bushman doctors say that sickness is a dirty nail, thorn, or arrow that must be removed. The voice spoke again, "These tweezers can also be used to attach the ropes to people, pulling the thread through their skin." In the vision, I asked my Hungarian friend Dezsoe Birkas, a medical doctor, if his father, who also had been a medical doctor, had a pair of those tweezers I could borrow and bring into the spiritual realm. (Later Dezsoe actually presented me with his father's tweezers that I still have today.)

Hillary and I were shown many spiritual wonders and marvels on our journey. We were taught that we could bring others to the classrooms with this vehicle. I had been told many years ago that it was possible to help others spiritually travel; now I realized that the Chrysler would make this possible. We went back and loaded all the mentorship students into the spiritual car that had enough room for everyone. We took them to the spiritual classrooms.

Each student was sent to a different place. I recall one man being sent to a spiritual mill where he made holy flour and his wife was baking it as spiritual bread, pulling it out of an old oven—both high spiritual anointments. I trembled when I saw another person sent to be among the disciples. One woman was given a flute and told to walk into the ocean. Her eyes remained above the surface of the water while she played the flute under the water. I witnessed everyone being dealt with and sent somewhere. I helped attach ropes all around a young man's body, preparing him for an ascent. A woman doctor we know was thrown into the body of an octopus to absorb its effortless movement. Another student was sent to a classroom where his eyes were covered while he was taught how to hear and feel holiness. Some were sent to the crossroads to learn how to pray and mourn. Some hearts were washed clean. Others were sent to specific classrooms. I recall that one of our friends wanted to go to the Kalahari, but knew not to ask. He was then suddenly sent there and when he arrived he jumped with glee. His wife received a crown of thorns, all filled with *n/om* that are ready to enter the recipient when it is time. On and on this went until we came back to ourselves with deep thanksgiving. I also brought back a new car: it's always waiting for another trip to mystery.

Church of the Holy Apostles

A few weeks after our first mentorship class graduation, one of our students, Joe, visited a spiritual classroom. Here is his report:

I dreamed that I was in my hometown, La Grange, Indiana, walking down High Street, where my best friend lived. Between a church on the corner of Michigan Street and the house on High Street was a very tall and disproportionally skinny church that I had never seen before. It was made of dark brown bricks and was obviously very old. I was in a stupor of disbelief because I had been down that street what seemed like a million times and had never once seen a church.

I walked up the steps to look inside and a woman hurriedly came out. I asked her about the place and how long it had been there. She somewhat gruffly told me the church was closed and to come back in a few hours because there would be a service at that time. I managed to peek inside and saw beautiful stained glass with classic orthodox iconography. She walked away and left me standing at the doorway.

It was only a minute (not hours, like she mentioned) when either the pastor or the music director came and invited me in. I noticed that the choir was rehearsing. The pews were made of wood, with a kind of dingy carpet on the floor, but the icons and stained glass were out of this world. When you looked up, you could not see the ceiling because it was so high.

I started talking excitedly to the priest, almost as if drunk, saying, "I grew up here and I have never seen this church. My best friend lives right down the street and I have a key to his house. I walk by here every day." He said that it was the Church of the Holy Apostles and that it had been there forever. I asked him why I had never seen it before and he laughed and answered, "You can't see heaven, either." The priest announced that the choir was rehearsing an old song that had lyrical lines in it from a letter of St. Paul. I bristled, since I tend to go back and forth on whether St. Paul brought more help or harm to Jesus.

At the same time, I was laughing inside myself because I was actually standing in a church that was both Orthodox and Protestant, and getting ready to hear a song with either a lost or mistranslated passage from St. Paul. The lyric was, "The fire is drawn, and the sticks are prepared, let us go now and tell the world and hold nothing back." I woke up very happy with tears of joy.

Joe's dream exemplified how the mystical ceiling was getting higher in the lives of our mentorship graduates. The lyrics from St. Paul he dreamed actually refer to the time that St. Paul made a fire from sticks and the heat from the fire woke up a poisonous snake hiding inside the sticks, which then bit him: "And when Paul had gathered a bundle of sticks, and laid them on the fire, there came a viper out of the heat, and fastened on his hand"(Acts 28:3). When people saw Paul bit by the snake, they regarded it as proof that Paul was a criminal, like a murderer, and that divine justice had sent the serpent. However, to everyone's surprise, the snakebite did not hurt him; he was delivered from all harm. Paul repelled the "censures and reproaches of men, and looked at them with holy contempt" (Acts 28:5) — that is, he shook off the viper and threw it into the fire.

When your soul is set on fire by the divine, nothing can harm you. You have nothing to fear as long as you remain inside the room that has a high ceiling, a place that only appears when the sacred flames are blazing. Once the fire is drawn and the sticks are prepared, do not hold back. Enter the church and join the choir. In the big room of First Creation, a poisonous viper is no match for a musical piper.

Entering First Creation

Hillary once had a vision that she and I were walking together in the Kalahari:

I looked down at the sand while I walked, never taking my eyes off the ground. We soon heard the sound of a women's dance in the distance and headed toward it. When Brad and I arrived, the women were standing around the fire, singing and clapping. They were dressed in colorful skirts and scarves. I noticed that this was not a typical dance. The women began teaching me something that cannot be easily described in words but only conveyed while under the influence of ecstatic song, movement, and the vibration of *n/om*. The women began to change form, moving in and out of their bodies like pulsing waves. They were showing me how to enter First Creation.

When you step into the big room of mystery, whether it's presented as a mystical church or Kalahari dance ground, you step into "the changing," what the Bushmen also call First Creation. This entry brings an incredibly strong physical vibration into your body that, when strong enough, alters your sensory perception. We are not referring to the kind of experience precipitated by a hypnotic trance induction, a workshop-taught "shape shifting" technique, or the neuro-biological effect of taking *ayahuasca*, psychedelic mushrooms, peyote, or LSD. Stepping inside First Creation brings a qualitatively different kind of mystical experience that surpasses the popular fantasies of having a vision or being in an altered state. Rather than something "seen" by the mind's eye, it is felt deeply as a radically different kind of emotion in which all your senses combine and become heightened until you feel as if you are dissolving into your surroundings. You become the rhythmic waves of music and dance, and this vibrational experience makes you resonant, sympathetic, and connected with God. The ultimate spiritual experience always involves vibration rather than conversation, musical notes rather than words, and clashing cymbals rather than interpreted symbols.

As an undergraduate student I recall my professor, Huston Smith, explaining in a lecture how he had hoped that taking psychedelic drugs would give him a full-blown mystical experience, something that had eluded him. He concluded that while drugs can help induce something similar to a religious experience, hallucinogens seem to not guarantee the kind of conversion that leads one to live a religious life. On the other hand, the utmost mystical experience that brings you closer to God more readily fosters the kind of radical change and rebirth that forever leaves you altered. While afterward you will continually go up and down the divine rope, you will not be the same person you were before the holy fire got into your bones.

The changing of First Creation is found by stepping out of Second Creation into First Creation, what we call moving from the small room of self to the big room of God. It matters less whether you swallow a plant powder or say a prayer; it is the size of the room that determines whether there is enough space for the divine to be present. Inside First Creation, a communion wafer may be more powerful than a mushroom, a joke may be holier than a magical incantation, and a song may be vaster than a massive cathedral. Entry into First Creation requires passage through the holy gate and this is often as small as the eye of a needle. Admission can't be purchased and there are no shortcuts. Nothing less than surrendering all is what takes you into the passageway of the First Creation birth canal, and you will never be delivered without a song.

The Dill Pickle Club

After many weeks of spiritual cooking intensives and visits to high spiritual classrooms, Hillary had a dream of a different sort. She and I were in a car that pulled into a single parking spot in the middle of a vast and blank landscape. There were no other cars, people, or buildings around. She continues the account:

174

The moment I pulled into the parking spot I looked up and noticed there was a parking sign directly in front of us that read, "This spot reserved for members of the Dill Pickle Club." I was extremely excited to point out the sign to Brad, remembering that he had previously told me the story of the Dill Pickle Club in Chicago. We jumped out of the car and rejoiced that we had finally received confirmation of our membership. When I walked around to the back of the car, I noticed there was a long name on our license plate that I didn't recognize: *Szukalski*.

The Dill Pickle Club (sometimes spelled "Dil Pickle Club") was a Bohemian club in Chicago, Illinois between 1917 and 1935. The club was founded and owned by Wobbly John "Jack" Jones. A theatre, speakeasy, and bohemian gathering place, the Dill Pickle Club was part of the "Chicago Renaissance." Located in Tooker Alley, the entrance had a "DANGER" sign placed over its orange colored door that was lit by a green light. On the door itself was written, "Step High, Stoop Low and Leave Your Dignity Outside." Another sign just inside the entrance advised, "Elevate Your Mind to a Lower Level of Thinking." Once fully inside, guests found a large main room with a performance stage. The Dill Pickle Club was frequented by all kinds of liminal characters including activists, performers, literary figures, and other radicals of their time. Its final demise came when it attracted too many mafia gangsters causing its authentic, Bohemian spirit to vacate.[125]

When Hillary woke up from the dream, she Googled the name "Szukalski" and discovered that it referred to Stanislav Szukalski (1893–1987), an artist, a key figure in the Chicago Renaissance, and a friend and collaborator of the Dill Pickle Club's founder, Jack Jones. Szukalski maintained a studio nearby. Originally from Poland, Szukalski was a formidable sculptor and painter who, after enjoying success in the United States and later Poland, was forced to flee Europe with his wife during WWII, moving to California, where he eventually fell into obscurity. Actor Leonardo DiCaprio had known Szukalski as a boy via his father, George DiCaprio, an underground comic artist who had been introduced to Szukalski by the artist's friend and patron, Glenn Bray. Leonardo DiCaprio and his father later sponsored an exhibit of Szukalski's work at the Laguna Art Museum in 2000. Fans of Szukalski considered it a tragedy that such a talented artist remained largely unrecognized and uncelebrated in the United States after WWII. Most inspiring to us was the discovery that Szukalski was a kind of mystic whose core message, written in a borrowed typeface from a dead language, meant "Help Yourself to the Sacred Fire."[126]

Know that Sacred Ecstatics sometimes benefits from a "dill pickle" state of mind, a departure from the mundane and sometimes over-serious piousness of spiritual practice. To help yourself to the sacred fire, leave your dignity, filigree, and trickster calligraphy outside in order to meet the minstrelsy of a wiggly ministry whose timpani sounds the polyphony of infinity!

The creative life force is always moving and changing, entering and then vacating the gathering places radical enough to host its fleeting presence on the stage. Honor the poets, artists, writers, and rabble rousers throughout the cosmos who keep the embers burning, ready to ignite the next brief renaissance. Stay on the lookout because the creative spirit often reawakens in the least expected places, and many geniuses of past, present, and future go largely unnoticed and unrecognized in this world.

Dr. Fulford Helps Heal Another Doctor

I woke up one morning after a powerful visit to a spiritual classroom. The dream was so real that I was momentarily convinced I had experienced it while awake.

> I was with Dr. Robert Fulford, the late renowned osteopath, and we discussed healing at great length. He then invited me to observe him work. All of the patients I observed were children and the sight of his kind and gentle way of being with them made me weep in the dream. Dr. Fulford said he had finally discovered that only one treatment mattered. He placed a hand-held vibrating device on the back of each patient, directly behind the heart. He said thinking too much about any trauma and trying to treat it at its presumed site of impact or injury was inefficient and unnecessary. "Just open the heart this way. All sickness is an injury of the heart; it is the underlying core of whatever else appears to be going on. Go to the heart and open it."

I wondered why I was being shown this and it then came to me that I needed to advise a particular person to have someone pulse his back daily with a vibrator placed directly behind his heart, just like Fulford had done in the dream. I immediately got out of bed and went to my laptop and found an email from that person, who is a medical doctor. It was an urgent plea for healing. He had composed the letter while I was dreaming:

> Dear Brad,
>
> I'm writing to get your wisdom, guidance, and perspective on things. I pray I am ready to receive it . . . The experience of living has gotten harder, not easier. The peaks and valleys of change are getting more erratic and severe. The minute I find a foothold, the footing then seems to crumble . . . my sense and experience of suffering is growing. It is a massive

internal pressure in my head, in my body, made so much worse by the leaden immobility that in-casts me and shrouds me in darkness.

The thing with it all is that I am getting really tired of being tired. Although my thoughts at these times dwell on fantasies of dying and suicide, I know in my heart that I won't act on them. Sometimes I blame my own cowardice for this. That being said, there are so many nights of late that I consider going to hospital (even though I know they have nothing to offer) just because it seems like the only answer in the here-and-now of my life to the pleas of: "I want to be healed," "I want to feel well," "I want to be whole," "I want to live," and "I want to be free from suffering." The thing is, in all of this, I am still a believer in healing, but that belief is faltering when I apply it to myself. You and I know of stories of great healing and stories of great healers (I am of course writing to one right now), but is that healing available to me?

I have the existential angst of a sailor, cast a drift in the Doldrums, no breeze to refresh or direct, no currents to move with, no fresh water to quench the unrelenting thirst of parched days and unrequited nights of longing to be made whole. . . . Please help me create a momentum to escape the grips of the gravity that continues to hold me down in immobility. Help me. . . . I am just hoping you can help point the way back to my own remembrance of that which is eluding me in this moment.

Thank you my Friend and Captain,

Love,
W.

After receiving his letter, I immediately wrote to Willis about what had taken place in the spiritual classroom with Dr. Fulford and gave him the prescription. He wrote back:

Dear Brad,

Thanks for feeling the depth of my feeling on this one. It is from the heart.

Amazing, as I was writing and hitting "send," you were dreaming. I thank all that is holy and a great confirmation in spirit. There was 35 minutes difference between when I hit send and you hit reply. No coincidence!

We started with the massage unit on the back of the heart this morning and it was a very joyful exchange with my lovely wife.

Thanks to the Spirit and thanks to you my friend for being available and open in the Spirit.

Blessings to you and Hillary,

Love,
W.

A month later he wrote again:

Hello Brad and Hillary,

Good news! I have to tell you I feel the best I have felt in years—good energy and minimal pain. The turning point was that night when you dreamed of Fulford. We are using a percussor on the back of my heart daily. I have started back to karate for the first time in 12 years—I love it. Built a small sweat lodge in the back yard just to heat things up. I also started a group session with my patients, myself included as

Chief Crazy. I have felt really energized in it and hence highly vitalized. It feels a bit what I imagine big-wave surfing to be—the thrill of riding a fine edge knowing at any moment you can lose your balance, go over the falls, be smashed up by the weight, then held under in the wash. How great is that? Anyway thanks for your prayers and not giving up on me. I am enjoying the sun while it shines. It feels great to be back.

Love,
W.

Many of the healers we have known also received prescriptions for their patients in vision. It is always up to God when, how, and for what patient such directives will be delivered. If a prescription comes directly from the rope to God it is wise to act upon it, even if you don't understand it. We give thanks to the Almighty for touching our dear friend's life.

The Floor Has Received New Nails

When I mourned on the Caribbean island of St. Vincent, I dreamed I was a small child living in the parsonage in which I grew up in Smithville, Missouri. I was lying in my bed, praying so hard that my pillow came out from under my head. It then stood straight up and floated directly over me. When I woke up and got out of bed in the dream, the nails from the walls starting coming out. Nails were flying everywhere and the whole scene was surreal, like something you might see depicted in a Hollywood movie. I learned that prayer has so much strength that it can actually pull the nails out of the walls and floor of your house.

While in Hollywood I dreamed that Hillary and I were taken to the living room in my grandparents' house. The wood floor had been removed so that an intricate structure underneath it could be seen. We noticed what a strong foundation the house had and commented that when the wood floor was placed back, there would never be any fear about its security. We then noticed that the structure had been attached to the foundation with brand new silver nails. The old nails in the house had been removed and replaced with brand new silver nails. Only one old nail remained.

This visit to a spiritual classroom took place after we had experienced numerous intensives in Europe that were spiritually on fire. Many people were receiving nails of *n/om* and visions were pouring through us. We accepted the visionary teaching as confirmation that the ground floor was ready to host the advancement of Sacred Ecstatics. New shiny nails of *n/om* have secured the sacred foundation, yet the work shall never be complete; there is always another person waiting to receive a new nail. The sacred ground must continually be made more secure so it can endure and forever welcome everyone home.

The Ropes Are Back

I went to a visionary classroom with Hillary last night. We were taken to a religious liberal arts college.

A woman guide arrived and said she wanted to show us something very special—relics recently collected and secretly put on display. She then mentioned that they were held in the Department of Literature. The campus was built on a hill, and the building she took us to was very tall and made of red bricks. Inside was a gigantic room with a ceiling higher than a cathedral. A long bar was suspended high in the air and ran from one side of the room to the other. It was holding what the guide said were the oldest representations of Jesus. Two wealthy benefactors, an older couple we later met on the tour, had made it possible for the college to acquire these sacred objects.

When we looked up, we saw that the right side of the bar held a collection of extraordinary ropes hanging from it. Each rope was one of a kind and had its own uniquely crafted small wings attached to it. The display was incredibly beautiful. It was clear that the wings were artistic masterpieces and that the ropes were not ordinary ropes, but something as holy as could be imagined, something not of this earth.

The guide then insisted that we see the main relic, the largest one that they considered the primary work. It was held in the campus chapel. When we went into that building, it too had an extremely high ceiling. Someone mentioned that the ceiling was higher than the building itself. There the primary work of art was a rope suspended over the altar. Unfortunately the rope was hanging horizontally as it appeared one end had been yanked to the left and was snagged and entangled on a manmade hook. A tall man wearing a tan-colored work uniform walked down the aisle and climbed a ladder on the side to grab hold of the rope. He started pulling on it and rocking it back and forth. The rocking motion seemed to rock the whole church and the earth as well. His action finally freed the rope and it dropped into its right position, hanging vertically, as straight as can be. This was the largest rope we had ever seen in our lives. Its diameter was enormous. The longer you stared at it, the larger it seemed to become until you couldn't bear to stare at it any more. It made you weak in the knees to look at it. We finally noticed that the bottom of the rope was frayed and we could see many fibers and strands, or smaller ropes held inside it. These were individual ropes to God and they were now ready to be used again. The music began inside of me and I woke up hearing holy songs playing one after another throughout the rest of the night.

There is a unique mystical rope for each human being and it is born of the original mainline rope to God, the link to the big room of mystery. The individual ropes hang in the house of literature where they are surrounded by the timeless stories and testimonies told by the anointed ones. The main rope itself resides inside a sacred place where former attendants allowed it to become bent to the left, hung on a manmade hook. It has now been let down and is a straight line waiting to grab hold of you. Shake the churches, shake the synagogues, shake the temples, shake the ashrams, and shake every ceremonial place, space, and ground so all the ropes will be straight again. Hold on to your rope with all your life because its wings will carry you home.

The Signature

Not long after dreaming the ropes I had another vision in which I went to a cathedral-like spiritual classroom that had no ceiling. All that could be seen above were the stars. Inside this vast place I was taught more about divine mystery, especially about how to make it accessible to others.

At the end of the teaching a scroll of paper dropped from the sky and a giant hand with a pen reached down and signed its name, one letter at a time, with the last letter a musical note, slightly slanted:

I was reminded that the soundtrack to mystery is not merely background music; it is the main track on which to travel. Afterward, Hillary and I laughed as we joked that the correct pronunciation of the name "God" is actually "go note," since the divine signature received was the word "go" followed by a musical note. To go toward the divine, sing a sacred musical note—a "go note."

The Pipe Dream

Decades ago, I went to a visionary classroom where my grandfather came to me and said, "There is a pipe in Guadalupe." He also gave me an otter bag for holding a medicine pipe. Months later, I was given a pipe and otter bag by an Ojibwa medicine man from Canada. I continued to wonder about the words my grandfather spoke. In the world of mystery there are usually multiple meanings and multiple prescriptions for action that point to multiple realities. I wondered whether the pipe was more than the sacred pipe that is smoked. Is it also part of a holy pipeline? Is it the pipe organ in a Mexican cathedral honoring The Virgin of Guadalupe? Is it the musical pipe or flute that Jesus played when he taught about the mystery of holy dance in the Gnostic Gospels and said, "I will pipe, Dance all of you . . .?" Is it the pipe that delivers holy water in a spiritual classroom? Is it the hollow pipe each of us is called to become?

Last night the pipe returned. I was sent in vision to the high school from which I graduated. There I found a pipe coming up from the ground that went through various valves before connecting the main line to the high school's pipes. Lying on the ground near it was a piece of a special luminous pipe, barely over a foot long, unlike anything ever seen before and definitely not of this world. If you looked at this pipe, you'd have the feeling that you recognize it—that you once received it, that you worked with it, that it was/is/shall be yours, and that you may have even placed it there on the ground.

In the dream, several days passed and I returned to see a crowd of people surrounding the pipe. It had been discovered. I started to approach the scene, but instantly sensed that it was better to not be seen near it. I could see that people were not pleased at the discovery of this mysterious object. It was unknown to them and they worried about its influence and whether the world would dramatically change because of its return. The police and FBI were investigating the scene. This is when I remembered that my fingerprints were on that pipe and that I could never do anything to catch their attention because it would link me to the luminous pipe. I knew the authorities would stop at nothing to prevent others from knowing what the pipe might do in the hands of its owner.

The price of having held and known and received the

luminous pipe is that you are forever linked to it. The spiritual mission you are called to fulfill must be very carefully accomplished, with the least attention drawn to yourself. Holy work requires the invisibility of self. The pipe itself will always rest near a holy place. Nothing can interfere with your spiritual closeness to it. Drawing unnecessary attention to yourself threatens the opportunity to use the pipe in the destined manner. The pipe carries many things across many realities, including delivery of crude spiritual oil, refined spiritual oil, holy oil, holy water, and holy smoke.

The pipe resides in the highest mystery, yet it is close at hand. Paradoxically, the more you effectively use it as intended, the less people are able to see you. The more people notice you next to it, the more distant from the pipe you risk becoming. You already know how to be invisible and get the job done—how to do what needs to be done without causing unnecessary distraction. You also know how to draw too much attention to yourself.

When near the sacred pipe, do not fill the room with too much chatter. That only draws trickster's attention. Do not show off what you know or that you are familiar with the pipe. Do not take all the oxygen from the room. Be less noticed. Let the pipe do what it needs to do. Get out of the way so mystery may flow and be felt. Now is the time to be the wisest you have ever been. Draw the least attention to yourself as you move closer to the luminous pipeline. Again, the less you are noticed being close to the pipe, the closer you are to it. When eventually you get so close that you disappear and become the pipe, no one will notice except God. On those occasions when something happens through you, it will be seen as God's fingerprint and not yours.

Coming Home: Living Behind the Highest Bars

After dreaming night after night in Hollywood, we felt guided to sell our house. This partly came about because we wanted to make our rope to God as strong as possible, putting everything we have on the line to better allow the divine to lead us. We wanted no unnecessary material imprisonment, so we sold our house and placed our few belongings (a piano, recording equipment, four chairs, books, art, and clothes) in storage. With this leap of faith and plunge into the unknown, we found visionary guidance touching our work in new ways.

Our foundational book, *Sacred Ecstatics: The Recipe for Setting Your Soul on Fire*, had been released to the public a few months before we left Hollywood. Soon after, however, we felt called to rewrite the whole book. For nearly six months we were sequestered in a rented room, editing and rewriting the book over and over again until we felt we had done all we could to serve a clear exposition and evocation of ecstatic spirituality. During this time we received reports from people throughout the world whose lives had been changed by our intensives and sessions. While we were grateful for how divine mystery personally touched our lives, we were even more thrilled to find that Sacred Ecstatics was doing the same to others.

One night I was sent to a classroom where an old blind man, a fortune-teller, asked me to sit down so he could read my future. He said these words, "Soon you will be behind bars." I woke up remembering the teaching of Paul, who was imprisoned in a Roman jail. Although he underwent tremendous suffering through frequent floggings and exposure that brought him near death, he was able to declare, "For Christ's sake, I delight in weaknesses, in insults, in hardships, in persecutions, in difficulties. For when I am weak, then I am strong" (2 Corinthians 12:10). This didn't mean that it was always easy, for there were times of tremendous hardship that brought him to the brink of despair. Paul discovered that the suffering each of us is given is our personal cross, our crossroads, just the amount of burden we are able to carry. It both breaks us and readies us to be made more whole. Suffering is not solely a negative, evil thing (nor an enemy, misfortune, or disease to conquer and eradicate); it is also a spiritual gift that enables divine alchemy to take place, transforming physical pain into spiritual gain, shifting the risk of losing your health to the good fortune of gaining spiritual wealth. Suffering enables the impossible to become possible, including the miracle of walking through the valley of the shadow of death as a means of ascending the mountain of eternal life. As Paul said, "I can do everything through him who gives me strength" (Phillipians 4:13).

Paul wrote letters to his parishioners, showing them how filled with joy he was during the darkest times when he lived behind the iron bars of a man-made prison. He was not downcast and filled with fear; he was an upbeat beacon of hope. He had known the best of times and the worst of times, and was able to conclude, "I know what it is to be in need, and I know what it is to have plenty. I have learned the secret of being content in any and every situation" (Philippians 4:12). He rejoiced that his truest home was found inside his heart where no one could destroy it.

Like Paul, your mind must wisely build sacred ground within your heart. Rejoice when your heart becomes a vast home without boundaries. Inside its center, all things in heaven and earth are brought together, and all walls of separation between you and God are broken and removed. In the midst of God's love, there is no anxiety, worry, or concern because newborn peace releases everlasting joy. As we learned through Beethoven, behind the highest bars of music, no prison bars can ever harm you. May your heart and mind be forever guarded by the infinite caretaker, forever illumined by the heavenly sunshine, forever fed by the holiest bread, forever sung by the composer of all life-changing songs, and forever loved by the greatest divine mystery.

Set on Fire

Years ago, right after Hillary I first met and were assigned to teach together in a graduate program in San Francisco, I had a dream that I went to an ancient monastery high in the mountains.

> There I was given a different mind, along with a smaller body that was the size a child. My eyes were made larger and more open—more able to absorb what was around me. After this mind and body transformation, I was led to the Dalai Lama. He too appeared smaller like a child. His eyes were also large and ready for absorption. There were many people in line to see him. A rather hysterical tall and thin older woman was in front of me. She seemed overwhelmed by the occasion and lost the ability to walk. I had to help her be seated until others could hold her. The whole scene seemed ridiculously exaggerated to me and I was not impressed by what was taking place.
>
> My turn finally arrived to meet the Dalai Lama. I sat on the ground in front of him and fully opened my eyes so we could each have a deep look at one another. I was surprised to see that he seemed slightly dissociated and lost, perhaps a result of the large number of people he had to meet. He was present in a rehearsed kind of way, but not in tune with the unique particularities of the situation. He proceeded to mumble some patter about Buddhist practice. I interrupted and said, "Look again." He bent over and opened his eyes even further as I did the same. Then the Dalai Lama reached out with his finger and touched me. This time he said, "I push on you to see what is inside you, but in your case, there

is nothing inside. You have no foundation. You are nothing." He suddenly became curious to know more about the deeper nature of "nothing" and asked his attendants to bring over a bucket of blessed water. The Dalai Lama sprinkled some of this water over my head and my head immediately caught fire. He then asked for the whole bucket to be poured over me. As soon as the water was poured I burst into a great fire. It engulfed the Dalai Lama and he was burned to ashes, but he was unharmed and still alive. My head was as hot as heat can get, but I felt no pain. I had no thoughts; I only felt the heat of the transformative fire.

After the burn, I noticed that the Dalai Lama's teachers were hovering over him as my parents were observing me from a slight distance. My father just watched without showing any excitement. I heard the Dalai Lama announce to his followers that he had just learned that "Nothing is a fire. Emptiness is the fire of creation."

At that moment in the vision, I began teaching. Words poured forth. I spoke with no desire to impart a particular understanding, but only to set others on fire. I saw a philosopher nearby trying to philosophize, but he could not hide that his primary desire was to appear like an expert. I looked at him and said, "I will not step into your dialogical form. That is your habit and it is not my purpose to fit into your way of staying the same. My lineages are Samurai *seiki jutsu* and Bushman *n/om*. I am not here to dialogue with you. I am here to set you on fire."

I woke up and my head actually felt like it was on fire. The heat was extreme, though strangely it was not painful. I felt reborn. I was different. I was not the same, though I was the same person. Something had been burned away. Perhaps everything had been burned away. My mind, heart, and soul were at peace. Since that dream, I no longer feel in control of the events of my life. It is handled by divine mystery. I have no attachment, no expectation, and no plan. I am a fire of nothing. I am a nothing that is on fire. This does not mean a thing. It is not about meaning. It is about burning, that is, being alive in the fire of the divine. I recall saying to myself, "I shall see how the world responds to my being a fire of nothing."

The next morning I shared this visionary report with our students by posting it in our virtual classroom. One of the students, Julie, replied:

> I feel as though I should feel shocked, surprised, and blown away by your post above, Brad. And yet, I am not. Last night, just before bed, I painted a painting. I do not know why—I was sitting down to paint something entirely different. I wanted to paint a woman, yet I painted a man. I wanted to paint ice, yet I created fire. I wanted to place that fire in the belly, yet it belonged on the head. The image came through me, not from me. Yes, it seems as though I needed to paint you with your head on fire.

Of course there are many times when I continue to be chilled by small-room thinking and filled with the concerns and worries that arise when hanging out in that kind of constrained space. The difference is that I now am more easily reminded that nothing can be solved or resolved in any small room. Forget finding help in the small rooms of coaching, therapy, psychology, philosophy, and even overworded religion; greater understanding of the meaning of words and concepts is not what you need. You must go where the holy water can be poured over you and set you on fire. In that big room, you are spiritually cooked and made ready to help set others on fire.

When one person is spiritually ignited, it is socially contagious. Anyone near such a person can also burst into mystical flames. The extent to which you are warmed, heated, or set on fire is determined by how empty you are. It is this nothingness that is combustible. Any inner or outer appearance of knowing cools you off and makes it more difficult for you to spiritually burn. One of the disadvantages of your living in the present epoch of human history is that there are too many opportunities to be fed all kinds of knowledge. A lot of it is mixed up and often perpetuates the opposite of what it professes to teach. Most so-called spiritual books, workshops, training, and the like help you become full rather than empty and lack the ecstatic fire that burns away all unnecessary mental baggage. Such teachings paradoxically make you an expert in how to be cold and full of pretentious knowing that includes feigned humility, rehearsed calm, artificial peace, passionless compassion, and compassionless passion. It's the equivalent of eating tons of junk food and finding yourself fattened yet malnourished. To set yourself on fire, you need to make more room inside for combustion to take place, which is only made possible by welcoming nothingness rather than any fullness of knowing it all.

We find that mentorship students who come to us emptier than others are most likely to be spiritually set on fire. Those who come full of all kinds of spiritual knowledge are usually at a disadvantage because they must do more work to become emptier. One advantage of growing up in the Kalahari of old was that there were no libraries full of best-selling popular books that help trickster lead you astray. Furthermore, there was no cultural norm to seek wisdom and well-being through greater insight, understanding, and elaborate explanation. All teaching and important transformation in the Kalahari took place around a sacred fire with song, rhythm, dance, and fully cooked teachers.

You need to find that fire. Make sure you leave your presumed knowing and posturing far behind so they won't stand in the way of your being cooked in the flames.

As mentioned early on, one of the great resources Hillary brought to our mystical work was her emptiness, cultivated by both her personal experiences of tragic loss and her spiritual relationship with Zen Buddhism. When we met, she quickly entered the sacred fire and journeyed to and through the experiential roots of the lineages that hold Sacred Ecstatics. Her mastery of handling and sharing ecstatic fire is inseparable from her constant dedication to maintaining an inner bowl of emptiness. As I witnessed her become an equal holder and teacher of this work, I was also brought more deeply into the heat and its corresponding emptiness. I was not ready to teach until we came together. Perhaps it has always been true, though sometimes forgotten, that spiritual teaching is best held in relationship. Human beings, after all, become emptier when they surrender to the greater whole of a relationship and it allows more room for individual differences to dance with one another. More importantly, as was taught long ago, only when two or more are gathered will the spirit be amidst them.

When the Walls Crumble, the Songs Pour In

I went to a classroom where Hillary and I were getting ready to go to sleep. I looked at the walls and they appeared so thin that huge sections of the wall were missing, revealing the outside where others were gathering. At most, there were only a few strips of old wallpaper dangling in the wind. I mentioned to Hillary in the dream that we are now living more exposed to the world. We felt both liberated and imprisoned by this realization. It seemed we were locked into this work in an inescapable way. While this was reason for jubilation, it was also challenging to come to grips with how our life was no longer ours to own. We had become prisoners of God. As the old spiritual "The Old Ship Zion" was heard, I felt more deeply than ever that we were most at home on board the spiritual ship that sails the divine sea, packed and ready for whatever destination is on God's itinerary.

This spiritual is a traditional African American "camp meeting" song that dates back to slavery times. Sung slowly and with deep sacred emotion, the lyrics invite you to have no fear and board the sacred ship that will release you from suffering and take you home. Here are some of the lyrics (the first line of each verse is typically repeated three times):

'Tis the Old Ship of Zion
Get on board, get on board

It has landed many a thousand
Get on board, get on board

Ain't no danger in the water
Get on board, get on board

It will take us all to heaven,
Get on board, get on board

Shortly after that vision I went to another spiritual classroom.

There I saw four mighty walls, the walls from the four directions that separate us from the spirit. As songs flooded my heart, I saw all these walls suddenly collapse and crumble, as holy spiritual water was released and poured forth with tremendous power. The songs I heard were "Have Thine Own Way Lord," followed by "I Surrender All."

"Have Thine Own Way Lord" was written by Adelaide A. Pollard in 1907. She went to a prayer meeting, frustrated and feeling "a distress in her soul" because she felt called to go to Africa but had no funding to get there. At the prayer meeting she heard an older woman pray, "It really doesn't matter what you do with us, Lord — just have your way with our lives." Inspired by that line of prayer, she went home and composed the song:

> Have Thine own way, Lord!
> Have Thine own way!
> Thou art the potter,
> I am the clay.
> Mold me and make me after thy will,
> while I am waiting, yielded and still. [127]

When you are with physical pain, place your hands on your body and pray, "Have Thine own way, Lord." When you emotionally suffer, place your hands on your heart and pray, "Have Thine own way, Lord." When you are lost and seek guidance, point to God and pray, "Have Thine own way, Lord." When you pray for your loved ones, open your arms and pray, "Have Thine own way, Lord." With this constant prayer, pray that God be the potter and mold you as clay.

When the walls begin to crumble and finally come tumbling down, the songs of sweet surrender arrive to carry you to the sacred sea. You will join those before you who also found ultimate joy once they handed their lives over to the Big Holy. Judson W. Van DeVenter wrote the lyrics to the song "I Surrender All," published in 1896, at the moment of his own surrender:

> For some time, I had struggled between developing
> my talents in the field of art and going into full-time
> evangelistic work. At last the pivotal hour of my life
> came, and I surrendered all. A new day was ushered

into my life. I became an evangelist and discovered down deep in my soul a talent hitherto unknown to me. God had hidden a song in my heart, and touching a tender chord, He caused me to sing.[128]

We pray that everything in your life be held and steered by God. Surrender all, knowing that when you do, the sacred songs will begin to flood your daily life and nighttime dreams. God has hidden a song deep down inside your heart. Let the walls that separate you from divine mystery crumble away. When this happens, a tender chord will be touched and a song released.

The Gossett Family

One of our mentorship students, Evan, had a sacred vision the same night I envisioned our worldly walls crumbling. His report:

Last night I dreamed that my girlfriend and I were with Brad and Hillary, having dinner on a train before they went off on further travels. After they left I immediately got word that Brad and Hillary were going to be hosting a night of teaching, telling stories about "the Gossett family," who I understood in the dream was an old-time religious Christian family of some kind. I went to where the Keeneys were teaching and found everyone gathered outside under a big tent.

The next morning Evan did some research and discovered there actually was a Gossett family. They were traveling evangelists in the United States and Canada. The father, Don Gossett, was a preacher, but a book—*Stubborn Faith: Celebrating Joyce Gossett*—had been written about his wife, Joyce Gossett (1929–1991), by their daughter.[129] Of particular interest is a section called "Eleven Lonely Months," written by Joyce herself. In it she notes that she received instruction from God to write the testimony "in order to help others." Joyce testifies that she was healed of a nervous breakdown when she was nineteen years old through prayer and song. She says that the most important thing in the healing of her "nerves" was the internalization of Scripture, moving it from a surface-level mental understanding to a deeply felt, "living" relationship with its teachings. Joyce writes:

> I read every book, the Scriptures, and sang every song I could find about Jesus. I searched for Him in His Word, in others, at every turn. I carried His Word with me to my job daily. . . . The pattern of my thinking became saner as I spent time in the Word of God. . . . I was feeding on the Scriptures. How real they were! Living, vital, literally for me. . . . I learned to act, to embrace them as my very own, His promises to me. I held onto His every saying, as clutching for my very life. . . . My life depended on this. . . . I could never stress [enough] the importance of knowing the Word of God as a living force in our lives.[130]

It was Joyce's personal experience with making Scripture come to life that likely inspired her to give this advice to her husband, Don, who faithfully prayed every morning:

> I suggest one of these mornings you make a tape recording of your hour-long prayer. Then instead of going through all the rigors of praying like that every morning, you could just turn the record on and let it play . . . honestly you say the same things every morning in exactly the same way, and it's just an hour of repetition.[131]

Moving from "an hour of repetition" to an hour of transformative prayer requires heating up your prayers with sacred emotion. As Joyce describes it, only when we "feed" on sacred words as holy bread can they become a "living force in our lives." Raised in a Pentecostal family, Joyce was a self-taught pianist who applied this same ecstatic know-how to music. As Gossett's daughter wrote of her mother:

> Her piano style was the classic Gospel or evangelistic style, with lots of arpeggios and fills up and down the keyboard. . . . Mom regarded "flowing in the anointing" keyboard style nearly as important as the preacher's words for setting the atmosphere for the "great transactions of faith in the Holy Spirit."[132]

Hold onto the core teaching of Joyce Gossett. In her deepest time of need she focused on heating up her prayers and songs so she could absorb, digest, and internalize them. Pay attention to how she advised her husband to pray in a more expressive way. Let "flowing in the anointing" arrive so that the atmosphere is conducive for being struck by divine thunder and lightning. Be stubborn with the kind of faith that sweeps away unnecessary distractions and makes room for sacred teaching to become a living force in your life.

Swallowed by Mystery

I dreamed one night that I looked out the window and saw an incredibly large bear, at least thirty meters high. It came running toward me at an impossible speed and in a split second instantly swallowed me whole. I woke up shaken and remembered that this is how an Arctic shaman is made in East Greenland — being eaten by a gigantic spirit bear. I prayed and fell asleep again.

When I later woke up and checked my email, I had received this letter from Agnes, one of our friends in Budapest:

> I had a dream last night. In my dream, I was walking around the city center. I passed by a park when I

suddenly stopped and saw a brown blanket on the ground. When I stepped closer, I saw a black samurai sword lying on the blanket. No one was near it, so I wanted to look around and see if someone was selling it. To my surprise, I wasn't able to move. My movement was frozen as if I was paralyzed and could only stand staring at the sword. I felt something in my stomach and in an instant the sword inhaled me. I was swallowed by that sword and disappeared. I was like a wind. I woke up and my whole body was shaking. I felt warmth on my spine and was so disoriented that I had to vomit three times. All day I was dizzy and could not get a song out of my head. Two days later, the song hasn't gone away and I can't get over what happened.

A mystical sword swallowed Agnes as a bear swallowed me. What Agnes didn't know was that she received a full transmission of the sacred vibration and will never ever be the same again. More specifically, we recognize that Agnes received a transmission of *seiki*, the Japanese word for the sacred vibration and mystical, vital life force. Hillary and I hold the *seiki jutsu* lineage of the late master Ikuko Osumi Sensei.[133] The practice and transmission of *seiki jutsu* dates back to old samurai Japan, and *seiki* itself is sometimes metaphorically described as a wind that circulates throughout one's body. It was a wonderful blessing to us and to Agnes that she received the incredible gift of *seiki* in this mystical way.

The swords, bears, sacred Harts, poets, song catchers, mystics, shamans, *seiki jutsu* masters, and saints are waiting for you to enter the big room where mystery is ready to swallow you whole. Rather than wait to do this on your deathbed, why not choose to do it on your life bed? It is our prayer that you will decide sooner rather than later to reach for your rope to God.

Every Time We Say Goodbye

In a dream Hillary and I were sitting in a cafe when a song was heard in the room. It was so beautiful that we stopped talking and went into a complete state of awe. The song absorbed all our attention and time literally stopped. When I was able to speak again, I said to Hillary, "What an amazing song!" She responded in kind. Then we noticed it was happening to everyone in the room. Even the waitress stopped and stood with a gaze of delight as the song touched her heart. When she came to, she also exclaimed, "What an amazing song!"

Here are the lyrics to the song heard in the dream, composed by Cole Porter in 1944:

Every time we say goodbye, I die a little,
Every time we say goodbye, I wonder why a little,
Why the gods above me, who must be in the know,
Think so little of me, they allow you to go.
When you're near, there's such an air of spring
    about it,
I can hear a lark somewhere, begin to sing about it,
There's no love song finer, but how strange the
change from major to minor,
Every time we say goodbye.[134]

Love brings the ultimate joy of togetherness that also carries with it the eventual heartbreak of separation. Whether it is your relationship with the people you love or your relationship with God, there is a constant bittersweet movement between coming together and pulling apart. Remember that the universe and everything inside it, including you, is a breathing song. The constant change from major to minor and back again, though strange, is the music of sacred change. It is climbing up and down the rope to God.

The Water Has Been Released

In a visionary classroom I saw Hillary and myself with a gathering of our students in a teaching room.

> All of a sudden water started pouring in. We looked up and there was a pipe sticking down vertically from the ceiling and water was gushing from it. The pipe was about four inches in diameter and extended about a foot from the ceiling. There was no valve to turn it off. It was clear to me in the vision that the pipe went straight to the sky, all the way to the heavens. Sacred water continued to fill the room. We tried catching and holding the water in a big metal tub while filling buckets to take it outside, but it continued to pour with no sign of stopping or slowing down. A voice was heard: "The water has been released."

At the time of this vision our mentorship students' lives were being flooded with mystery. People were receiving arrows of *n/om*, feeling the presence of saints and ancestors, and prayers were coming alive. Our students were also having powerful visions. Amy, one of our students, wrote Hillary this letter:

> I just woke up from a dream and my hands are shaking as I feel strong energy pulsing through my body. In the dream, I was at our mentorship gathering and we were all in a large circle. After you and Brad started teaching, I closed my eyes and felt a grip of tightness in my belly. I was pulled into the middle of the circle by a force I could not deny. My body started dancing, moving, and shaking on its

own. I then heard Brad shout, "Look up!" I immediately looked up and saw a column of white luminous energy that was about two or three inches in diameter. It felt like lightning was entering my body. (My hands are still shaking as I type this.)

In the dream, this energy came down from up high and it pulsed through me. I started to climb the column with my hands hanging onto the light beam. I moved upward and then was smoothly sucked up. I looked down and could see the ground below getting smaller. When I looked back up I felt totally consumed by white light. I then landed back at the middle of the circle of students at the mentorship, now shaking and looking straight at you and Brad. You then showed me how to ground myself.

The water has been released! The sacred fire is burning! Join the saints, shamans, mystics, healers, preachers, and teachers of old as they are walking, talking, singing, and dancing up the rope to God. Get on board, get on board!

Climbing the Song Ropes to Heaven

I often dream of hearing sacred songs and one I commonly hear is the old hymn, "Softly and Tenderly." Last night I heard its lyrics sung again: "Come home, come home. You who are weary come home . . ."[135] This song was composed by Will Lamartine Thompson, who started his career as a composer of popular music. Thompson was so successful that he was called the "Bard of Ohio" and the "millionaire songwriter."[136] One night he attended a revival service led by Reverend Dwight L. Moody, the same evangelist who influenced young Edgar Cayce. That was the moment he dedicated his life to composing hymns rather than popular songs.[137] One of Thompson's songs, "Softly and Tenderly," became a standard "invitation hymn" for churches, played at the end of a service to invite people to take a walk to the front of the sanctuary and pledge their life to God. In the final moments of Reverend Moody's life, Thompson visited him on his deathbed. The famous preacher said, "Will, I would rather have written 'Softly and Tenderly Jesus is Calling' than anything I have been able to do in my whole life."[138]

Though you can imagine, meditate, and contemplate any spiritual matter, you will never feel like you are actually taken to the heavens unless you sing and climb the rope to God. All the visions we have shared provide testimony and teaching about how to make this climb. In summary, you must clear the ground and sweep away the dust to make room for the rope to appear; then walk toward it and hold on with all your life; and finally, you must sing to get yourself launched. Without a song, as we have repeatedly advised, you can't go up the rope in a whole-hearted and whole-bodied way.

It should now be no surprise that the Kalahari Bushmen regard the rope to God as a special kind of powerful song that when sung in the right way enables you to climb all the way to the sky village. Such a song is the ultimate gift from God and it, more than anything, is what you need in order to transform suffering into joy, and move from being lost to being forever found. It carries you across the sacramental bridge between heaven and earth, and when you climb the rope to God, you are set on fire and spiritually cooked. This is the journey that establishes a true mystical, shamanic, and ecstatic spiritual life.

You can't take voice lessons and learn how to sing in a way that helps you make the mystical climb. Neither musical talent nor professional training has anything to do with accessing this mystical–musical means of spiritual travel. Something mysterious has to happen to you. God must touch a tender chord in you and perform a mystical operation on your windpipe so it can become a hollow pipe through which sacred song can pass. This is the same pipe through which the holy water can flood your life with spiritual blessings. It is also the rope that tugs on your heart to come home to God. Though this rope has many forms in First Creation, it is above all else the pipe that makes music for the highest mystery dance. Yes, there is a pipe in Guadalupe and there is a luminous pipe that is waiting for you. Some people vision that such a pipe or rope is attached or sewn to their body. God will choose how the divine hookup will be made, but have no doubt about this: when you make contact with divinity, the somatic–spirit divide is crossed and you forevermore have a mystical singing voice and a spiritual concert hall within your heart.

You may also be given the gift of making rhythm or playing a musical instrument. In a vision I once found myself pregnant with a drum powerfully beating inside me. I actually gave birth to this drum in the dream as its rhythms soaked into my skin. I woke up able to play the drum in a spirited way. The same kind of visionary dream takes me to a mystical piano where I play in an enhanced kind of way. That is how my music grows and is blessed with more of what Joyce Gossett called a "flowing in the anointing." There is nothing more thrilling to me than to play the piano that resides in the big concert room of musical mystery. I am never able to even come close to playing the piano in the way that I hear it played in vision, just as Beethoven said he could only compose a fraction of the music he heard in the cosmos.

One of our favorite hymn composers is Fanny Crosby (1820–1915) who composed over 8,000 hymns, including several of our favorite songs—especially "Pass Me Not, Oh Gentle Savior" and "Blessed Assurance." Crosby said of her hymn-writing process:

> My verses come without the slightest effort, as though someone were singing them to me. I retire at night with a theme or a strain of music on my mind; in the morning there is the complete song, stanza by stanza. I have really felt at times that the angels had

been talking to me.[139]

When songs arrive like this in dream, they are made holy and spiritually empowered for the dreamer. When subsequently shared with the world, these songs become sources of spiritual nourishment for others as well. It matters not whether the song is an original composition or one with which you are already familiar. If deeply felt to the extent that it spiritually shakes and bakes you with its sacred vibrations, then be assured that you have mystically received a song, a rope that enables your windpipe to become a vessel for divine expression and transmission of God's blessed assurance, grace, and love.

In the early 1920s a man named, Thomas A. Dorsey, was a leading blues pianist known as "Georgia Tom." He later became known as the father of black gospel music and his composition, "Precious Lord, Take My Hand," is one of our cherished visionary song-ropes. Dorsey, like everyone else, had to be broken before he could be made ready for spiritual work. After becoming the pianist for the great blues singers Ma Rainey and Bessie Smith, one night he noticed an "unsteadiness" enter into his playing. It grew worse and persisted for two years, leaving him unable to compose or perform. He considered suicide and had a nervous breakdown. Dorsey sought the help of numerous doctors, but they could find nothing wrong with him and no treatment eased his suffering. Finally, he visited a faith healer named Bishop H. H. Haley, where he had an unexplainable experience that changed his life. Dorsey, in his biography, states that Bishop Haley pulled a "live serpent" out of his throat and told him, "Brother Dorsey, there is no reason for you to be looking so poorly and feeling so badly. The Lord has too much work for you to let you die."[140] After he was healed, Dorsey decided to devote his life to sacred music.

Later, in the worst tragedy of his life, his young wife died in childbirth, followed by the death of their child the next day. In that despair, Dorsey said he finally became "a channel through which God spoke."[141] That is when the music and lyrics of "Precious Lord" poured into him:

> Precious Lord, take my hand,
> Lead me on, let me stand,
> I am tired, I am weak, I am worn.
> Through the storm, through the night,
> Lead me on to the light,
> Take my hand, precious Lord, Lead me home.[142]

Perhaps you have never sung before, or at least not in public, or you think it is impossible for you to sing in a sacred way. In truth, the less you think you can sing, the better prepared you are for God to anoint your voice. Such a miracle happened to a saintly man named Cædmon, who lived in England and died sometime between 670 and 680. Though regarded by many as a saint, he was never formally canonized. He was an illiterate cowherder who miraculously became able to perform a song of creation in Old English verse. As reported by Bede (an historian during that era and author of *Ecclesiastical History of the English People*[143]), one night Cædmon attended a feast where a harp was being passed around so that each person could contribute a song. Because he was unable to sing, Cædmon left the party and likely felt ashamed.

After this, while sleeping in a cattle shed, Cædmon had a dream in which a mystical stranger appeared to him and commanded him to sing a song. When Cædmon responded that he could not sing, the stranger (variously depicted as a man, an angel, or a piebald cow) insisted and said, "Nevertheless you must sing to me," implying there was no doubt that Cædmon could sing. When asked what he should sing, the stranger replied, "Sing. . . about the beginning of created things." When Cædmon received this answer, he immediately started to sing "verses which he had never heard." The next morning he could remember every detail of his dream; furthermore, he was able to recite additional verses beyond what he had heard. Soon scholars arrived to evaluate his gift. The Abbess St. Hilda, believing he had received a divine anointment, decided to test Cædmon's powers and gave him a partial verse of sacred history, asking him sing the whole of it in song. Cædmon fulfilled the request by the next morning when he sang an inspired original verse. Hearing this, the abbess sent him to be a monk at a monastery. For the rest of Cædmon's life, learned scholars would tell him scriptural stories and he would convert it to sung poetry, making it come to life in a vivid way.[144]

As another historian noted, this transformation enabled the scripture to pass "out of its old Latin into its new English dress, out of the dim seclusion of cell and school to the open sunlight of the English countryside, and from the narrow limits of the parchment-scroll to the wandering minstrelsy of the vernacular poetry."[145] Cædmon, in other words, moved the scripture off the page and into the English pasture, making it more accessible to people in a way that touched their hearts and transformed their souls. No other poet was said to be able to bring a scriptural story to life like Cædmon, "for he was divinely aided, and through God's grace received the art of song." Bede also notes that Cædmon was described as "inflamed with the heat of great zeal"[146] and when he sang, he had no control of himself. This Northumbrian peasant–poet from England's Dark Ages brought a new sound into the world.

No matter what others might suggest or want to believe, the oldest mystical and shamanic truth of spirituality concerns how the ecstatic performance of music is what forms the connection between human beings and the gods. There is no other way than to trust and obey the anointed flow of sacred music — the soulful rhythms and melodic lines that are able to take hallowed words on a spirit-powered ride. Hitch a ride to the crossroads on a song and then have that song, as well as your voice and any other instruments, become anointed, infused, and blessed by holiness. Only then can your mystical life truly begin, granting you a ticket of admission to the grandest concert of all, with songs that welcome and embrace your return home.

Diamond in the Sky

One night I was sleeping in a tent in the Kalahari and I dreamed that a shooting star fell from the evening sky. Just before it hit the earth, I saw my father in a baseball uniform running for that star. He leapt high into the air and caught it.

My father loved baseball and he was good enough to be given a letter of intent from the St. Louis Cardinals when he was fifteen years old. Unfortunately, he never made it to the big leagues because he was enlisted to serve in the war. I was fortunately able to watch him make a great play in the Kalahari night. I woke up after that dream and went outside to take a look at the sky. That moment I saw a shooting star exactly like I had dreamed it. I felt my father by my side.

The next morning I told my Bushman friends about the dream and they became very excited. They explained that this kind of dream, followed by the actual sight of a falling star, means that you have received a special ancestral rope to God. You can find your way to God through the love you have for your ancestors. You only need one felt connection to one other person that feels like a deep familial love, whether it is through a father, mother, grandfather, grandmother, sibling, or other relative. Even a spiritual parent or brother or sister will work; this includes a teacher or preacher. They, in turn, have the same kind of link to someone else. One link at a time, the chain, the rope, the pole, the tube, the ladder, or the staircase to First Creation heaven is made. As the Bushman way teaches, the rope to God consists of all your ancestors holding on to one another or dancing while slumped over one another's backs, as they like to depict it.

Last night I prayed while wondering whether I would receive a dream that would help move our book toward an ending.

Hours later I found myself in a vision getting into the Chrysler Imperial to begin another journey. Hillary joined me and we drove on and on for quite some distance. We finally pulled up to an old baseball stadium that looked like it had been built in the early 1900s. We parked the car and went into the entrance to the stadium, which was a tall, concrete tower that appeared like a control tower found at an old airport. We climbed the steps to the top where tickets to the baseball game were being sold. The game had already started and I could hear the wonderful cracking sound of a bat hitting the ball as the crowd cheered on. I asked the man at the booth what tickets were still available for the game. He said, "You are in luck because we have the best seats in the house, box seats behind home plate, unless you'd like to sit behind first base. We have those tickets as well." I received our tickets and Hillary and I went through the gate. Somehow we, and the whole stadium, were suspended in the heavens. There I beheld one of the most beautiful sights I have ever witnessed. I stood directly behind home plate, high in the sky, looking at the most magical baseball diamond in the cosmos. I could feel my father waiting for me to be by his side. As we walked to our seats, I woke up and felt blessed that I had come home.

The ancestors and all the holy saints, mystics, shamans, healers, preachers, and teachers of old are waiting for you to join them in the diamond in the sky. Start at home plate and hold your pipe, now a First Creation bat that is ready to swing with just the right rhythm, and hit the ball on the mark that sends you to first base. Make sure you round all the bases and find yourself completing a victory lap, bringing you back home to the beginning, ready for the next swinging hit that sends you on another trip around the diamond in the sky.

Only You

As these visionary experiences continue coming to us, Hillary and I trust that we are being led day by day, as we never stop praying that God's will be done. In spite of any practical frustration that arises in everyday affairs, we deeply feel we are walking and dancing with those former mystics, saints, shamans, healers, teachers, and preachers who moved toward the divine. This gives us the ecstatic joy that forever makes us want to sing.

> One night after praying with all my soul, I dreamed we were walking in the plaza of an old New Mexican town. We were startled to hear a young man's voice singing at the top of his lungs. As we came closer to the music, we discovered that the singer was Hillary's late brother, Brett. He was singing the song "Only You," popularized by the Motown-style group, The Platters. It was so enthusiastically and sincerely performed that it opened both our hearts and brought tears of joy.

Hillary was not surprised when I told her that I had dreamed of Brett singing in this way, because he had a been a musician and a singer all his life. In high school he was chosen to sing the national anthem before the football games, and was well known for the way he belted out a song, something I didn't know before the dream. Hillary was very close to her brother in her childhood, but he died in a tragic car accident when he was nineteen years old. The words to the song spoke to what is true about her relationship with him, our relationship with one another, our relationship with all our beloved ancestors, and our relationship with the divine:

> Only you can make all this world seem right
> Only you can make the darkness bright
> Only you and you alone
> Can thrill me like you do
> And fill my heart with love for only you
>
> Only you can make all this change in me
> For it's true, you are my destiny
> When you hold my hand
> I understand the magic that you do
> You're my dream come true
> My one and only you[147]

We end with this song ringing in our hearts. We thank God for being the one who makes the most important changes and highest visions come true. Only the divine changing of First Creation can alter your misdirection, set you on course, and take you to your destiny. May you find the truth that makes darkness bright and turns wrong to right.

No matter how lost you are, know that there are four directions—the existential bases surrounding you. This is the diamond of perfect mystery where each step brings you closer to home. We sincerely and faithfully call upon the name of all that is hallowed, praying that you be made hollowed and ready to receive all the gifts God has to offer. We exclaim, "Thank you!" with a leap of joy, celebrating and honoring all the ancestors, especially the original First Father and First Mother from whom we all came and to whom we forever belong. And to you, we finally sing with the mystical chorus from on high, "Only you can make God's dream come true."

AFTERWORD:
THERE IS NO LAST WORD

The visions continue.

Last night I dreamed Hillary and I were on a panel at a public conference on spirituality. A couple of well known popular teachers had just spoken about how to be a better human being. There was nothing that they said that was new, nor was anything mentioned that would inspire a debate. It was the tone in which they spoke that seemed to negate whatever truth they tried to convey. I heard someone next to us whisper, "They use spirituality to float their own boat, don't they?" We turned to see who had said this and noticed that an old man who had been sitting next to us on the panel was getting up to take a break. We decided to join him and when I stood up to leave I noticed that I was slow to move. I was reminded that I, too, was becoming an old man. The three of us left that stage and went somewhere private where we could be away from the crowd.

We all sat down in another room and looked at each other. We weren't sure what to say, though we knew exactly what we all felt. It was the same discomfort Hillary and I experience whenever we are within earshot of most of the popular spiritual teachers; it makes us want to flee in the other direction. Then at the same moment in the dream, all three of us spontaneously shouted the same words, "That was awful!" and immediately broke out in laughter. I did not know who this other man was, though he looked familiar. As I examined him, his appearance seemed to change. I thought he might be Philip Kapleau, or Gary Snyder, or Robert Aitken, or perhaps Alan Watts who was purposefully changing his expression to be playful. Though I couldn't settle on his identity, there was something I wanted to say to him. I rambled on about what Hillary and I had learned over the years about mysticism. After sharing this with the old man whose name I could not remember, I leaned over and said, "My point is to make sure that you forget what I said. Don't let any teaching get in the way. Make sure you are always empty."

I then fell asleep again, only to enter another dream.

In an old Japanese monastery, an elder handed me an empty bowl and asked, "Is this the answer?" Without thinking I replied, "No." He asked, "Is that your answer?" Without saying anything, I smiled and said nothing as I deeply realized that there is no question. Rather, there is only the *quest* that must *shun* whatever distraction or obstacle is found on the highway to earth-as-it-is-in-the-vastest-heaven.

Later, when I shared the dreams with Hillary, she reminded me that the Zen master Nyogen Senzaki (teacher of Robert Baker Aitken) wrote that his grandfather taught him "to live up to the

Buddhist ideals outside of name and fame and to avoid as far as possible the world of loss and gain."[148] You too should run far away from any teacher who values name and fame, especially if they emphasize the world of loss and gain. I looked at archival photos of old Zen teachers and found the old man I had seen in my dreams. When I showed the image to Hillary she was delighted because it was Taizan Maezumi Roshi, founder of the Zen Center of Los Angeles where she had once lived.

Cooked spiritual testimony and teaching provide a broom that helps sweep away the dust accumulated from whatever was previously said. The words will never stop, nor will the accumulation of dust and the need to sweep. You must constantly clean the dirt off the floor, the shelf, the books, and the words before you can climb the rope to utmost mystery. Remember that the rope is also the long stick of the broom and the sacred spine that holds together the pages of each holy book. We pray that our testimony will help you discover that God has always had a hold on you. That is the only story you need to remember so you can tell it and retell it over and over again.

ENDNOTES

[1] The Keeneys, *Sacred Ecstatics: The Recipe for Setting Your Soul on Fire* (Createspace, 2016).

[2] Ibn al-'Arabi, *al-Futuhat al-makkiyya* (Cairo: Bulaq, 1911), 1:153–54.

[3] Gopi Krishna, *Kundalini: The Evolutionary Energy in Man.* (Boulder: Shambhala, 1971).

[4] José A. Argüelles, *Charles Henry and the Formation of a Psychophysical Aesthetic Chicago* (Chicago: University of Chicago Press, 1972), 24–25.

[5] Ibid., 155-156.

[6] Ibid., 156.

[7] Bradford Keeney, *Aesthetics of Change* (New York: Guilford Press, 1983).

[8] Thomas Mails, *Fools Crow: Wisdom and Power* (San Francisco: Council Oak Books, 1991), 18.

[9] Bradford Keeney, ed. Profiles of Healing, 11 vols. (Philadelphia: Ringing Rocks Foundation and Leete's Island Press, 1999–2004).

[10] Bradford Keeney, *Bushman Shaman: Awakening the Spirit Through Ecstatic Dance* (Rochester, VT: Destiny Books, 2005).

[11] John Woo, director, *Windtalkers*, film (United States: Metro Goldwyn Mayer, 2002).

[12] THIRTEEN/WNET New York, *Religion and Ethics Newsweekly* (transcript and video), August 31, 2007, http://www.pbs.org/wnet/religionandethics/2007/08/31/august-31-2007-circuit-preacher-david-brown/912/.

[13] Ibid., par. 5.

[14] Ibid., par. 20.

[15] Keeney, *Aesthetics of Change*.

[16] Bradford Keeney. *The Flying Drum: The Mojo Doctor's Guide to Creating Magic in Your Life* (New York: Atria Books and Hillsboro, OR: Beyond Words, 2011).

[17] Geoffrey Farthing, *Exploring the Great Beyond: A Survey of the Field of the Extraordinary* (Wheaton, IL: Quest Books, 1978), 88.

[18] The Keeneys, *Sacred Ecstatics*, 235.

[19] William S. Burroughs, "Cut-Ups: William S. Burroughs" (YouTube video), May 21, 2011, https://www.youtube.com/watch?v=Rc2yU7OUMcI, 1'16".

[20] Dan Shepherd, prod., "Cutting Up the Cut-Up" (documentary broadcast), June 25, 2015, BBC Radio 4, http://www.bbc.co.uk/programmes/b05zl52m.

[21] We use *The Holy Bible*, King James Version (New York: American Bible Society, 1999).

[22] John Bunyan, *The Pilgrim's Progress* (Philadelphia: Charles Foster Publishing, 1891; Abbotsford, WI: Aneko Publishing, 2014).

[23] Dante Alighieri, *The Paradiso*, trans. John Ciardi (New York: Penguin Books, 2001), Kindle ed., canto XXXIII.

[24] Philip T. Nicholson, "The Soma Code, Parts I-III: Luminous Visions in the RIG VEDA," *Electronic Journal of Vedic Studies (EJVS)* 8, no. 4 (2002), accessed February 17, 2017, https://www.researchgate.net/publication/303897480_The_Soma_Code_Parts_I-III_Luminous_Visions_in_the_RIG_VEDA, 47.

[25] Isabelle Robinet, *Taoist Meditation: The Mao-Shan Tradition of Great Purity* (Albany: State University of New York Press, 1993), 110.

[26] Henry Reed, *Edgar Cayce on Channeling Your Higher Self* (New York: Warner Books, 1989), 223.

27 W. Y. Evans-Wentz, ed., *Tibetan Yoga and Secret Doctrines: Seven Books of Wisdom of the Great Path* (Oxford: Oxford University Press, 1958), 193.

28 Stephen Hirtenstein, *The Unlimited Mercifier: The Spiritual Life and Thought of Ibn 'Arabi* (Oxford: Anqa Publishing and Ashland, OR: White Cloud Press, 1999), 122–23.

29 Emilie Zum Brunn and Georgette Epiney-Burgard, *Women Mystics in Medieval Europe* (St. Paul, MN: Paragon House, 1989), 89–90.

30 More on this topic can be found in Chapter 6 of the Keeneys' 2016 book, *Sacred Ecstatics: The Recipe for Setting Your Soul on Fire.*

31 Bradford Keeney, ed., *Hands of Faith: Healers of Brazil* (Philadelphia: Ringing Rocks Foundation and Leete's Island Press, 2003).

32 Saint Teresa of Avila, *The Interior Castle: Or, The Mansions* (Charlotte, NC: TAN Books, 2011).

33 Paul Barnes, *Franz Liszt and the Sacramental Bridge: Music as Theology of Presence,* accessed January 18, 2017, 1, http://www.paulbarnes.net/pdfs/lisztsacramentalbridge.pdf.

34 From Heinrich Heine, "The Musical Season of 1844," republished in *Laphram's Quarterly* and accessed January 18, 2017, par. 3, http://www.laphamsquarterly.org/celebrity/lisztomania.

35 Barnes, *Franz Liszt and the Sacramental Bridge,* 3.

36 Ibid., 3.

37 Ibid., 4.

38 Ibid., 4.

39 Alex Ross, "Sacred Dissonance: John Adams's Passion oratorio, in Los Angeles," *The New Yorker,* June 18, 2012, pars. 1–3, http://www.newyorker.com/magazine/2012/06/18/sacred-dissonance.

[40] The Keeneys, *Sacred Ecstatics*, 113–14.

[41] Elliot Forbes, ed. *Thayer's Life of Beethoven* (Princeton: Princeton University Press, 1967), 1:496.

[42] Pierre Baudry, *The Truth About Beethoven's So-Called* Moonlight Sonata, May 8, 2011, 1, http://amatterofmind.org/Pierres_PDFs/ EUROPEAN_ART/BOOK_III/2._THE_TRUTH_ABOUT_BEET HOVEN'S_SO_CALLED_MOONLIGHT_SONATA..pdf.

[43] Lyndon H. LaRouche, "The Secret of Ludwig Van Beethoven," April 1977, par. 19, accessed March 21, 2017, http://www.schillerinstitute.org/music/2010/ lyn_1977_beethoven.html.

[44] Willi Apel, *The Harvard Dictionary of Music*, 2nd ed. (Cambridge: Belknap Press of Harvard University Press, 1969), 809.

[45] As quoted in Jocelyn Goodwin, *Music and the Occult: French Musical Philosophies 1750–1950* (Rochester, NY: University of Rochester Press, 1995), 205.

[46] Keller to New York Symphony, 1 February 1924, pars. 1, 4, 5, *Letters of Note*, March 27, 2014, http://www.lettersofnote.com/ 2014/03/my-heart-almost-stood-still.html.

[47] Baudry, *The Truth About Beethoven's So-Called* Moonlight Sonata, 12.

[48] Forbes, *Thayer's Life of Beethoven*, 1:305.

[49] "Isaiah 66:2—Gill's Exposition of the Entire Bible," Bible Hub, accessed March 20, 2016, par. 4, http://biblehub.com/ commentaries/isaiah/66-2.htm.

[50] Henry Osborn Taylor, *The Mediaeval Mind: A History of the Development of Thought and Emotion in the Middle Ages* (New York: The Macmillan Company, 1919), 1:485.

[51] This and subsequent quotes from Mechthild as quoted in Frank Tobin, ed., *Mechtild of Madgeburg: The Flowing Light of the Godhead* (Mahwah, NJ: Paulist Press, 1998), 6.13.

[52] Ibid., 6.29.

[53] Ibid., 3.3.

[54]Bob O'Hearn, "Mechthild of Magdeburg," *Western Mystics* (blog), March 24, 2015, pars. 6–19, accessed March 20, 2014, https://westernmystics.wordpress.com/2015/03/24/mechthild-of-magdeburg/.

[55] Harvey D. Egan, An Anthology of Christian Mysticism, 2nd ed. (Collegeville, MN: The Liturgical Press, 1996), 171, as quoted by Katherine Gill, "Selections from *St. Bernard's Sermons on the Song of Songs*: On the Song of Songs: Sermon 1," par. 19, accessed January 18, 2017, http://people.bu.edu/dklepper/RN413/bernard_sermons.html.

[56] S. O. Fawzi, *Mystical Interpretation of Song of Songs in the Light of Ancient Jewish Mysticism* (doctoral thesis, Durham University, 1994), 141–42, http://etheses.dur.ac.uk/1159/.

[57] John H. Livingston, *The Psalms and Hymns, with the Catechism, Confession of Faith, and Liturgy, of the Reformed Dutch Church in North America, Selected at the Request of the General Synod* (New York: W. A. Mercein, 1838), accessed March 20, 2017, https://archive.org/stream/psalmsandhymnsw01livigoog/psalmsandhymnsw01livigoog_djvu.txt.

[58] Hymnary.org, "The Blest Memorials of Thy Grief: Timeline," accessed March 20, 2017, http://www.hymnary.org/text/the_blest_memorials_of_thy_grief.

[59] Hymnary.org, "The Blest Memorials of Thy Grief: Page Scans," image 1, accessed March 20, 2017, http://www.hymnary.org/text/the_blest_memorials_of_thy_grief.

[60] Brian G. Najapfour, "The Piety of Joseph Hart as Reflected in His Life, Ministry, and Hymns," *Biblical Spirituality* (blog), April 11, 2012, par. 1, https://biblicalspiritualitypress.org/2012/04/11/the-piety-of-joseph-hart-as-reflected-in-his-life-ministry-and-hymns/.

[61] Joseph Hart, *Hart's Hymns* (London: Hawker & Co., 1911).

[62] Hart's autobiography can be found online. See Kevin Twit, "The Preface to Joseph Hart's 'Hart's Hymns' from 1759 Is a Classic in Spiritual Autobiography," Indelible Grace Hymn Book, October 7, 2013, http://hymnbook.igracemusic.com/resources/joseph-harts-preface.

[63] Ibid., par. 12.

[64] Ibid., par. 15.

[65] Ibid., pars. 17–18.

[66] Ibid., par. 9.

[67] Ibid., par. 22.

[68] Ibid., par. 22.

[69] Peter C. Rae, "Joseph Hart and His Hymns," *Scottish Evangelical Bulletin* 6 no. 1 (Spring 1988): 21, https://biblicalstudies.org.uk/pdf/sbet/06-1_020.pdf.

[70] Joseph Hart, *Hymns' on Various Subjects* (London: Hamilton, Adams, and Co., 1850), 138.

[71] Ibid., 148–49.

[72] Ibid., 23.

[73] Ibid., 31.

[74] Twit, "Preface to Joseph Hart's 'Hart's Hymns,'" par. 19.

[75] Ibid.

[76] Thomas Wright, *The Life of Joseph Hart* (London: Farncombe & Son, 1910), 1–4.

[77] Ibid., 20.

[78] Ibid., 20.

[79] Ibid., 21.

[80] Ibid., 23.

[81] Ibid., 25.

[82] Ibid., 4.

[83] Twit, "Preface to Joseph Hart's 'Hart's Hymns,'" par. 10.

[84] Ibid., pars. 10–11.

[85] Ibid., par. 12.

[86] Ibid., par. 12.

[87] Thomas Wright, *The Life of Joseph Hart* (London: Farncombe & Son, 1910), 34.

[88] Ibid., 34–35.

[89] Twit, "Preface to Joseph Hart's 'Hart's Hymns,'" par. 21.

[90] Ibid., par. 27.

[91] Ibid., pars. 18, 21.

[92] Ibid., par. 27.

[93] Edgar Cayce, *Edgar Cayce, My Life as a Seer: The Lost Memoirs*, ed. A. Robert Smith (New York: St. Martin's Press, 1997), 190.

[94] Ibid., 40.

[95] Ibid., 45.

[96] The lyrics were written by Mack Gordon for the 1942 movie *Iceland*. "There Will Never Be Another You," JazzStandards.com, accessed March 20, 2017, http://www.jazzstandards.com/compositions-0/therewillneverbeanotheryou.htm. Lyrics available from "There Will Never Be Another You," SongMeanings.com, accessed March 20, 2017, http://songmeanings.com/songs/view/3530822107859035291/.

97 We transcribed lyrics from a version of the hymn as sung by Robert Bradley Jr., a renowned gospel singer. See Praise Move, "J. Robert Bradley — Heavenly Sunshine" (YouTube video), April 14, 2012, https://www.youtube.com/watch?v=yoLUXeKVWxE.

98 Written by Lucie E. Campbell. According to this blog it was published in 1928. See bwimadmin, "Great Women of History: Lucie Campbell-Williams by Courtney Lyons," *Baptist Women in Ministry* (blog), May 18, 2010, http://bwim.info/ great-women-in-history/great-women-of-history-lucie-campbell-williams-by-courtney-lyons/.

99 Ibid.

100 Charles Walker, *Miss Lucie* (Nashville: Townsend Press, 1993), 156, as quoted in Pamela Palmer, "Lucie E. Campbell-Williams: A Legacy of Leadership through the Gospel," August 1, 2008, 19, https://dlynx.rhodes.edu/jspui/bitstream/10267/23978/1/200 8-Pamela_Palmer-Lucie_E_Campbell_Williams-Blankenship.pdf.

101 Hymnary.org, "Touch Me Lord Jesus: Full Text," verse 2, accessed March 20, 2017, http://www.hymnary.org/text/ touch_me_lord_jesus_campbell.

102 Robert Llewelyn, *Daily Readings with Julian of Norwich* (Springfield, IL: Templegate Publishers, 1985), 1:33.

103 One of the most studied Zen Buddhist texts is Dogen Zenji's *Tenzo Kyōkun*, sometimes translated into English as *Instructions to the Cook*. In it Dogen discusses the essence of Zen through the activities of the office of *tenzo*, or head cook. There are many translations of this text, including Ichimura Shohei's *Zen Master Eihei Dōgen's Monastic Regulations* (Washington: North American Institute of Zen and Buddhist Studies, 1993).

104 Bradford Keeney and Hillary Keeney, *Way of the Bushman: Spiritual Teachings and Practices of the Kalahri Ju/'hoansi* (Rochester, VT: Bear & Company, 2015), 115.

105 The lyrics were written by Frank J. Myers in 1982; see Myers, "Biography," par. 1, accessed March 20, 2017, http://www.frankmyersmusic.com/biography/.

106 C. Norman Shealy, *Energy Medicine: Practical Applications and Scientific Proof* (Virginia Beach: 4th Dimension Press, 2011), 97.

107 "The Round Dance of the Savior" (hymn from Acts of John), as quoted in Michael S. Howard, "The Round Dance — Text and Commentary," *Essays on Gnostics, One on Cathars* (blog) November 20, 2006, http://psychandgnosticessays.blogspot.com/2006/11/round-dance-text-and-commentary.html.

108 Seymour Bernstein and Andrew Harvey, *Play Life More Beautifully: Conversations with Seymour* (Carlsbad: Hay House, 2016).

109 Louis Fischer, ed., *The Essential Gandhi: An Anthology of His Writings on His Life, Work, and Ideas* (New York: Vintage Books, 1962), 168.

110 Poetry Foundation, "E. E. Cummings: [i carry your heart with me(I carry it in]," accessed March 20, 2017, lines 1–2, https://www.poetryfoundation.org/poetrymagazine/poems/detail/49493.

111 Antoine de Saint-Exupéry, *Airman's Odyssey* (Orlando: Harcourt Books, 1939), 195.

112 This popular quote is often attributed to Winnie-the-Pooh, but we were unable to locate the source.

113 This quote from *Oedipus at Colonus* can be found in John Bartlett, *Bartlett's Words to Live By* (New York: Little, Brown & Company, 2006), par 6.

114 As quoted in Anne Waldman and Lisa Birman, eds., *Civil Disobediences: Poetics and Politics in Action* (Minneapolis: Coffee House Press, 2004), 211.

[115] Elizabeth Barrett Browning, *Sonnets from the Porguguese: A Celebration of Love* (Readaclassic.com, 2009), 49.

[116] E. E. Cummings, *Etcetera: The Unpublished Poems*, ed. George James Firmage and Richard S. Kennedy (New York: W. W. Norton, 2001), 121.

[117] E. E. Cummings, *Selected Poems* (New York: W. W. Norton, 2007), 70.

[118] Kabir Helminski, ed., *The Rumi Collection* (Boston: Shambhala, 1998), 53.

[119] Thomas Merton, *Love and Living*, ed. Naomi Burton Stone and Brother Patrick Hart (Orlando: Harcourt Publishing, 1979), 27.

[120] Jack Kerouac, *Dharma Bums* (New York: Penguin Books, 1958), 244.

[121] In Margaret Ferguson and Mary Jo Salter, eds., *The Norton Anthology of Poetry, Full 5th Edition* (New York: W. W. Norton, 2004), 1190.

[122] Kimberly Wallace-Sanders, *Mammy: A Century of Race, Gender, and Southern Memory* (Ann Arbor: University of Michigan Press, 2008).

[123] Hymnary.org, "In the Garden: Full Text," verse 1, refrain, verse 2, accessed March 20, 2017, http://www.hymnary.org/text/i_come_to_the_garden_alone.

[124] Kenneth W. Osbeck, *101 More Hymn Stories: The Inspiring True Stories Behind 101 Favorite Hymns* (Grand Rapids, MI: Kregel Publications, 1985), 40.

[125] See Chicago Historical Society, "Dill Pickle Club Entrance, n.d.," *The Electronic Encyclopedia of Chicago*, 2005, accessed March 20, 2017, http:// www.encyclopedia.chicagohistory.org/ pages/3580.html; Marc Moscato, "The Tradition of Non-Tradition: The Dill Pickle Club as Catalyst for Social Change," 2009, accessed March 20, 2017, http://marcmoscato.com/wp-content/uploads/2009/04/preview.pdf; and Newberry Library, "A Brief History of the Dill Pickle Club," 2009, accessed March 20, 2017, http://publications.newberry.org/frontiertoheartland/ exhibits/show/perspectives/dillpickle/briefhistory.

[126] Vivan Letran, "DiCaprio Boosts Artist's Show," *Los Angeles Times*, August 19, 2000, accessed on March 20, 2017, http://articles.latimes.com/2000/aug/19/entertainment/ ca-6884.

[127] Kenneth W. Osbeck, *101 More Hymn Stories*, 112–13.

[128] Ibid., 135–36.

[129] Jeanne Halsey, *Stubborn Faith: Celebrating Joyce Gossett* (Blaine, WA: ReJoyce Books, 2011).

[130] Ibid., 36.

[131] Ibid., 50.

[132] Ibid., 108.

[133] See our book, *Seiki Jutsu: The Practice of Non-Subtle Energy Medicine* (Rochester, VT: Healing Arts Press, 2014).

[134] Lyrics can be found at AlltheLyrics.com, "Everytime We Say Goodbye," accessed March 20, 2017, http://www.allthelyrics.com/lyrics/cole_porter/ everytime_we_say_goodbye-lyrics-903837.html.

[135] Hymnary.org, "Softly and Tenderly Jesus Is Calling: Full Text," accessed March 21, 2017, http://www.hymnary.org/ text/softly_and_tenderly_jesus_is_calling.

136 Robert K. Brown and Mark R. Norton, eds., *The One Year: Great Songs of Faith* (Wheaton, IL: Tyndale House Publishers, 2005), 189.

137 Richard Neill Donovan, "Hymn Story: Softly and Tenderly," 2008, par. 7, accessed March 21, 2017, https://www.sermonwriter.com/hymn-stories/softly-tenderly-jesus-calling.

138 C. Michael Hawn, "History of Hymns: 'Softly and Tenderly Jesus Is Calling,'" par. 12, accessed March 21 2017, www.umcdiscipleship.org/resources/history-of-hymns-softly-and-tenderly-jesus-is-calling.

139 Darlene Neptune, *Fanny Crosby Still Lives* (Naples, FL: Neptune Ministries, 2001), 96.

140 Michael Harris, *The Rise of Gospel Blues: The Music of Thomas Andrew Dorsey in the Urban Church* (Oxford: Oxford University Press, 1992), 96.

141 The Faith Project, "This Far By Faith: Thomas Dorsey," 2003, "Precious Lord," par. 1, accessed March 21, 2017, http://www.pbs.org/thisfarbyfaith/people/thomas_dorsey.html.

142 African American Registry, "Take My Hand Precious Lord by Thomas A. Dorsey," 2003, verse 1, accessed March 21, 2017, http://www.aaregistry.org/poetry/view/take-my-hand-precious-lord-thomas-dorsey.

143 Judth McClure and Roger Collins, eds. *Bede: The Ecclesiastical History of the English People* (Oxford: Oxford University Press, 1969).

144 Ibid., 215–16.

145 Josephus N. Larned, *New Larned History* (Springfield, MA: C. A. Nichols Publishing Company, 1922), 999. https://archive.org/details/newlarnedhistory01larn.

[146] As cited in John Smith Russell, *The Ruthwell Cross, North Umbria, from about A.D. 680* (London: Micheaelsen & Tillage, 1866), 31–32.

[147] Genius Media Group, "Only You: The Platters," verses 1–2, Genius.com, accessed March 21, 2017, https://genius.com/The-platters-only-you-lyrics.

[148] Nyogen Senzaki and Ruth McCandless, *The Iron Flute* (Rutland, VT: Charles Tuttle & Co., 1961), 161–63.

Made in the USA
Middletown, DE
26 January 2020